GREEN MC

BY
ELLIOTT MERRICK

TRUE NORTH
FROM THIS HILL LOOK DOWN
EVER THE WINDS BLOW
FROST AND FIRE
NORTHERN NURSE
PASSING BY
GREEN MOUNTAIN FARM

ELLIOTT MERRICK

Green Mountain Farm

Vermont was named by early French explorers
who saw the north end of the Appalachian chain
and called the region *vert mont*, green mountain. It is blue sometimes, and also white.

The Countryman Press
Woodstock, Vermont

Copyright acknowledgments: Chapter 9 of this book was originally
published in *The New Yorker* magazine, 1937. Poem by Rachel Field on
page 132, copyright © 1934 *The New Yorker*.

Library of Congress Cataloging-in-Publication Data
Merrick, Elliott, 1905–
        Green mountain farm / Elliott Merrick ; foreword by Lawrence
Millman.
        p.   cm.
Originally published: New York : Macmillan Co. 1948. With new
foreword.
        ISBN 0-88150-435-1 (alk. paper)
        1. Merrick, Elliott, 1905–   —Homes and haunts—Vermont. 2. Novelists,
American—20th century Biography. 3. Historians—United States
Biography. 4. Farmers—Vermont Biography. 5. Depressions—1929
Vermont. 6. Farm life—Vermont. I. Title.
PS3525.E6394Z47   1999
843' .8—dc21   99–38142
                                                                          CIP

Published by The Countryman Press
PO Box 748, Woodstock, Vermont 05091

Distributed by W. W. Norton and Company, Inc.
500 Fifth Avenue, New York, NY 10110

Cover painting by Kathleen Kolb

Printed in the United States of America
10 9 8 7 6 5 4 3 2

FOREWORD

Remembering Elliott Merrick

TOWARD THE END OF HIS LIFE, Elliott Merrick, who died in 1997 just a few weeks before his 92nd birthday, often joked that he was "historical." He could recall the first Model T Fords hitting the roads; he wrote the copy for the first Dutch Boy paint cans; and he was one of the select authors, with Ernest Hemingway, F. Scott Fitzgerald, and Thomas Wolfe, of legendary Scribner's editor Maxwell Perkins. Even so, I thought of him as a contemporary. And he was never more contemporary than in his concern for the plight of Nature in an age dedicated to either paving it over or chopping it down. But he would have hated my capitalization of the word nature. For he hated pretension nearly as much as he hated human assaults on the environment.

Merrick was a man of immense good cheer and equally immense generosity, but also a man whose honesty could have a rapierlike edge. Concerning a writer on Arctic themes whose work he found blowzy and unreadable, he told me: "Her new book burned quite well in my woodstove." Every year around Christmas he'd send me a card beneath whose manger scene or beaming Santa he would scrawl "Isn't Christmas awful?" At the same time he was sufficiently romantic that he could tell me only half in jest that if I didn't like the novel *The Bridges of Madison County,* I was an "unfeeling wretch." He could be unfeeling himself on occasion, and yet, besides my own, there is no one I would rather have had as a father.

In 1929, Merrick—a young man in search of a geography he could call his own—went to Labrador. There, as a volunteer for the Grenfell Mission and later as a schoolteacher, he experienced one of the last true wildernesses in North America. Never mind that winter temperatures often plummeted to fifty or sixty below zero, or that there was no contact with the outside world for almost half the year. He had found his geography. And he would have been content to remain in this "pristine, beautiful land," (as he called Labrador) forever. But, as he later said, "A major in English literature from Yale and a minor in French did not prepare me for the life of a Labrador trapper."

Merrick and his wife, Australian-born nurse Kate Austen, returned to the United States at the height of the Depression. For a while, they lived in Manhattan and Merrick delivered Mrs. Wagner's Pies to greasy spoon diners in and around the city. At least he had a job, albeit one that could not have been farther removed from what he most wanted to do and where he most wanted to live (for Merrick, cities were, if not the devil's own spawn, at least pretty close to it). Meanwhile, he'd started selling stories about Labrador to *Scribner's Magazine*. With the money he earned from these stories, he bought a tumbledown farm in one of the few parts of the country, Vermont's Northeast Kingdom, that could ever be mistaken for Labrador.

He took up residence in Vermont at a time when small, family-run dairy farms were still the backbone of the local economy. Later, of course, the big milk corporations like Hood, Borden, and Sheffield would knock these little farms out of business, and a way of life stretching back almost to colonial times would be gone for good. But Merrick was lucky; he witnessed this way of life when it was still alive and mostly well.

From the beginning, he looked to Thoreau for guidance. "Live simply and naturally" was Thoreau's oft-expressed message. But the tenant of Walden Pond had had it easy, only once, in Maine, venturing into the wilderness he so eloquently celebrated. Merrick himself found Vermont a luxury compared to Labrador. "Having lived in tents when the temperature was well below zero, we could not believe that electricity and running water, or any of a thousand other amenities, were the essentials of a contented family," he wrote me.

Actually, he had no choice but to live simply, since he was nearly as poor as his Craftsbury Common neighbors (the town he calls Horseshoe in *Green Mountain Farm*).

He discovered his literary voice almost immediately, with *True North* (1933), a rhapsodic, lyrical paean to the Labrador wilds; this book so enthralled its editor, Maxwell Perkins, that he reputedly asked Merrick if there was anything *he* could do in Labrador. Merrick continued writing about Labrador in a fictionalized autobiography *Ever the Wind Blow* (1936), a long novel entitled *Frost and Fire* (1939), and *Northern Nurse* (1942). The last of these titles, reprinted in 1994 (The Countryman Press), tells of his wife's experiences as a nurse with the Grenfell Mission. It is perhaps the finest book ever written about the North from a woman's point of view.

Neither his writing or the farm paid the bills, so in 1939 he took a job as an instructor in English at the University of Vermont. The academic world was totally alien to his temperament. "Promise me that you'll never become a professor," he once told me in a grave voice, as if he were telling me not to become a serial killer. His dislike of professoring was genuine. Still, I can't help but think that he might have liked it more if he could have done it in some open-air setting, in the middle of a lake, say, or on a mountain.

During the war years, he worked for the Office of War Information in Washington, and while there he wrote a runaway bestseller—a pamphlet on the United Nations Merchant Marine that was dropped by the millions into occupied Europe. Later he became so curious about the merchant service (its men were unsung heroes compared to their naval counterparts, and he'd always liked unsung heroes better than the sung variety) that he shipped aboard a convoy tanker bound for bombed-out Liverpool. From this journey came a not very satisfactory novel entitled *Passing By*. But he was too personal a writer to be a good novelist. His best characters are taken directly from life. This includes a character named Elliott Merrick, too.

The University of Vermont did not renew his contract after the war, and he accepted a teaching position at Black Mountain College in North Carolina. A year later he took a job as a science editor at the Southeastern Forest Experiment Station in Asheville. And although he preferred editing foresters' prose to university teaching, he did not prefer North Carolina to Vermont, at least not at first. "In leaving Vermont," he told me, "Kate and I had such a sense of loss that we did not recover for many years." I suspect that part of the reason he wrote *Green Mountain Farm* was to retrieve something of value from his previous life in the Northeast Kingdom.

But *Green Mountain Farm* is not an escapist idyll. Quite the contrary. It is a crisp, unsentimental, often very funny book that deserves a place next to the poetry of Robert Frost and the fiction of Howard Mosher on the short list of the best writing about Vermont.

This is not a book that will teach you how to become a successful farmer. For that, you will need an agricultural manual and a dose of good karma. But it'll tell you all about the precarious existence of a writer ("You have to sidle up to a desk in a strategic way or it won't serve you"—excellent advice!), the joys of skiing by moonlight, and how to coax a hog into a pen. One of the best chapters is set nowhere near the farm, but on Lake Champlain, "that long jewel between the mountains," and gives an account of a transcendant canoe trip Merrick took with his wife. In fact, *Green Mountain Farm* is not so much about renovating a hardscrabble farm as it is about renovating the soul by contact with the natural world. Merrick, in writing it, gave the lie to the old adage that you can't go home again.

Over the years, he reconciled himself to North Carolina, especially after he created a Blue Ridge farm in Swannanoa more or less on the model of his Green Mountain farm in Craftsbury Common. But his writing days were over. Apart from a handful of brief articles, an extended essay on the disastrous Hubbard-Wallace Expedition in Labrador, and an unpublished book about sailing to Maine, he wrote practically nothing for the last fifty years of his life. It's almost as if the boreal realm, whether Labrador or northern Vermont, was his source of inspiration, and now that he was cut off from it, he was cut off from his muse as well.

By the 1970s and 1980s, a steady trickle of admirers was showing up at Merrick's door, some with copies of his books to be signed, still others seeking his wise elder's advice about their own northern peregrinations. I confess to being one of these pilgrims. And the man I met was briny with personality, remarkably young in spirit, and so passionate about the North that I felt like telling him, "Pack your bags, my friend, and get down your snowshoes. We're hopping the next dogsled for points north." And if it weren't for his advanced age, I'm convinced he would have done it, too. Done it in a trice.

So I would hop that dogsled without him. But if I encountered something unusual on a trip—an old Indian campsite, for example—I'd stash it in the berth that my memory reserved especially for him. And when I got back home, I'd ring him up. He would query me closely about what I'd seen, and maybe tell me that he knew the Indian camp from sixty years ago, when it was still occupied. Sometimes I would hear the rustling of a map in the background. He may or may not have been living vicariously through these conversations. One thing I do know, however: without him as an invisible sidekick, my own journeys in the North will seem less interesting. Much lonelier, too.

Not long ago I paid a visit to the farm Merrick wrote about in *Green Mountain Farm*. It was an unusually warm day for late fall, and a bluish haze was resting like threadbare cotton on the nearby hills. By the afternoon, there was a soft drizzle that did not feel wet so much as caressing. I watched a group of mergansers glide resolutely across Little Hosmer Pond as if they were on a mission of great importance. At one point I heard the tremulous wail of a loon sweep across the pearl-gray water. And I thought I could also hear a voice saying, as it once said in a letter to me, "Nature, love it or leave it, is really all we've got. Best to love it . . ."

LAWRENCE MILLMAN
CAMBRIDGE, MASSACHUSETTS
MARCH 1999

1

It SEEMED pretty impossible in those early days that we would ever have a farm. We had practically no money, my wife and I were both city bred, I had just been fired from my job as a truck driver, and it was in the depths of the great Depression of 1932. Prior to the truck-driving experience we had spent two or three years in the subarctic living with trapper people, and I suppose that had made us hardy. Anyhow, we wanted a farm, so we got one—small, rocky, rugged, and dearly beloved. That's the curious aspect of a farm: a farm supports you while you're winning it; even depressions, for all their train of ills, do bring the price of land down; and there are a lot of angles to a family farm that have little connection with economics, unless you want to make your definition of economics so broad as to include snow in the moonlight, blisters on the palm, and laughter and icicles. You can't really do your accounting in dollars and cents on a farm. They say, you know, that no small businessman can possibly compete with a farmer when it comes to losing money year after year and still staying in business.

About all we had to begin on was an idea. And we did just about everything wrong. The place we eventually picked was rocky, relatively infertile, full of steep, cut-up little fields that are hard to work. It is infinitely far from markets, in a land of savagely severe winters, and the growing season is about one hundred days. But it just happens that we like it and are happy on it, largely because it has some wildness to it. We did everything wrong, but it turned out right.

1

We struck out for Vermont, northern Vermont, largely because of its lakes and little roads and hills. At first we had to rent—a most undesirable procedure. It was an old black farmhouse in the shape of a letter L. We only used one angle of it, and even that part was in bad repair. We papered and painted and patched up the sagging porch, and we scraped and puttied and fussed most industriously, at first. The place had its points. It was high on a hill, looking straight across miles of Lake Champlain water to the peaks of the Adirondacks. The lake was five miles wide there, and among the massed blue peaks beyond were Whiteface, and Mount Marcy. Even better were the close-by wooded coves. Behind the house we looked across broad fields to the Green Mountains in the east—Camel's Hump, Mansfield. This magnificent estate cost us five dollars a month. We thought it was heaven on earth, but very few people shared this idea. We had arranged to have the Return Loads moving van outfit bring some of our sticks of furniture from New Jersey. It was a cold late November afternoon when the van rolled in across the grass. A couple of colored men climbed stiffly out of the cab, looked around and shivered. Gray clouds were scudding out of the west. The lake was torn with whitecaps, and the Adirondacks were a bunch of steel teeth way over on the New York side. The driver rolled his eyes expressively; in the falling dusk the effect was startling. "You all ain't a gwine to *live* hyar, is you?" he said, reluctant to open the doors of the van. But we reassured him, whereupon he and his helper set to work on the tables and chairs with dispatch. "We got to git outa hyar," he mumbled. And his helper added, "I sure be glad to get back to Hoboken."

We genuinely thought we were going to live there forever and ever in spite of the cold dreariness of that first autumn afternoon. There never was such a house with a view. Maybe we'd buy that old house someday. I had just sold my first book, and had an idea that I'd be rich and famous henceforth. As it happened, nothing could have been farther from the truth. The book came out in the middle of the Bank Holiday when people were busily losing their life savings and hadn't even the price of carfare, much less $2.75 for a book. As I look back, I'm amazed that we could so blithely have crossed our great Rubicon on a spiderweb. But it turned out to be one of those fortunate mistakes—one of those fraught-with-peril enterprises that you might never have embarked on if you had known the consequences—like being born, for instance.

Right away I must tell those kindred souls who want to go to the country too and start living that my being a writer had very little to do with our continued survival. Some years I made as little as 900 dollars, and a person can make more than that working on the roads. You don't *have* to be burdened with a writer's uncertainties and worries to get along in the country. If your talents are more stable and satisfying, so much the better. There are scores of ways to make a living in the country, and there are going to be more. In this age of electric motors, rapid travel, and communication, there are more opportunities in the country than there are in the city for enterprising men and women whose principal capital is independence and energy.

Gradually we found that that first house had most everything wrong with it. The plaster was falling out of the walls. The rainwater cistern leaked. The rickety chimney was one of those most frightful abominations of man, a diagonal one, in which the soot lodged solid, and our landlord, a farmer named Coonrod, took two months to fix it. Elmer Coonrod had the most wonderful old Model T Ford which he and his son-in-law used to ride about in, inspecting the broad clay plains of his two rented farms. Usually both back doors of the Model T were open to accommodate a dozen cedar fence posts laid in crosswise and sticking out. What he wanted two rented farms for I can't imagine, since he never did much of anything with either of them. Maybe he just wanted plenty of acreage as gamboling ground for his Model T.

We had a wood range in the kitchen and a heater stove in the

3

parlor. We had also a four-months-old baby boy. The snow got very deep, and the cold was intense, but we never felt lonely. The firewood I had cut in the late fall was green. We used to watch water steaming out of the butt ends of chunks. But we were happy there. It is a matter of temperament, you see. I was writing furiously, making practically nothing. From a money standpoint I might better have been driving a milk truck or trapping foxes. In the spring, even when the cellar filled up full of water to the seventh step, we were still happy. There is no spring like the soft blessedness of Vermont spring, because you've earned it. You've earned it twice, thrice, and quadruple. Place is very important to some people—physical surroundings, fields, water, the curve of a road, above all space. Robert Louis Stevenson says, "Certain dank gardens cry aloud for a murder; certain old houses demand to be haunted; certain coasts are set apart for shipwreck." Well, there are certain spots just made for us to live in, and we'd rather be poor there than rich somewhere else. It is all a matter of temperament. I have always, even as a child, had the feeling that I have only one life to live and I must live it in the country. When I was a kid, we led a highly suburbanized existence. But once a year for a month we took off to Maine and really lived. There we palled around with some walrus-whiskered fishermen in a place called Perkins Cove. The fishermen were never in a hurry. They took two days to tar a net if they felt like it. They didn't need to be in a hurry; they had the sea and the sunsets and the back country pine woods all year 'round. By the time I was ten years old I had come to the conclusion that the fishermen were much smarter than the summer folks. The fishermen had it all year for practically nothing, whereas the summer boarders worked tooth and nail to get a month of it.

The Coonrod shack had some fine features. One was the big well under the elm tree by the road. The story was that somebody dug and dug, and twenty feet down, not a sign of water, he struck a solid granite ledge. The soil being mostly clay in that part of the

4

Champlain Valley, veins of underground water are relatively scarce. This old well-digger was a persistent cuss, and having put so much work into his hole in the ground, he made one last gallant attempt. He drilled the ledge and stuck a charge of dynamite in it—when, lo, a stream of water as big as two fingers gushed out of the rock, "and it has never stopped from that day to this." When we came there the grand old well was cluttered in its muddy bottom with scythe blades, bashed milk cans, rotten leaves, broken bottles and rubber boots. Two of us, working like mad, bailed it dry, and one kept it dry while I cleaned all that stuff out of it. I hardly ever passed by the well after that without stopping to look down. It was like a clear, cool eye, and in the bottom, in the current, a few grains of sand were always doing a little dance to themselves, hidden away, twenty feet beneath the roadside.

We had our own rocky nook beside the vast lake too. It was a place of squarish ledges, like tiers of crooked terraces, leading down to the water. The way to this place from our house wound across the road and down through a grown-up field past an old fallen-in pig pen and through some trees. You came out of the trees to see the whole jewel-like lake below you, Lake Champlain of song and story, five miles wide at this point, and 130 miles long. Here and there on the steep terraces, which went down like gigantic natural steps, were thorny blackberry vines growing out of cracks in the rock, curved and carnivorous. They were not thick and impenetrable—just pointedly on guard. Storms roared like an ocean against the bottom terrace, throwing spray high up the rock. But on quiet days you could sit and dangle your feet over the stone and listen to the plunk-chunk of wavelets lapping in the chinks. Nobody ever went there except us. Nobody seemed to know the ledges were there or to care. Sunny days of rare warmth we sat above the water, Kay, the baby, and I. And we'd put our hands on the gray warm rock and feel that life is good. It is strange now to think how often we and no one else went there. Perhaps it was that we were so poor. We had no team of horses, no silo to fill, no

5

tractor to fix, no twenty cows, no apple orchards, no broilers to pluck, no 200 acres, no hogs. We were just a man and a woman and a child by the lake, and for some odd reason we were content.

The place was full of local characters, of course. The fact that we were immediately considered a bit peculiar ourselves gave us something of an entrée into the charmed inner circle. One of our favorites was Bolland Manvers, the village carpenter. He was something of a drunk, and used to have terrific fights with his wife. Perversely enough, we sympathized with him. As penalty for driving when drunk, he had lost his operator's license, and this in turn made his big, solid wife the family's only legal driver. The situation irked him no end. A skillful mason and carpenter, something of an architect and plumber, he traveled about the township extensively to his jobs. He was a great hunter and fisherman too, muskrat trapper, boat builder. What made him maddest was that when he wanted to go somewhere, he had to ask his wife to take him. She hated his drinking, and always used the transportation business as a threat against him. If you saw Bolland making a long hike along the road to work, you could be pretty sure that he had been hitting the bottle again and his wife was punishing him. However, he used to sneak out with the car at night now and then, as did a great many other licenseless youths and maidens in that township of blessedly unreconstructed eccentrics. Once when he was drunk and took the car, his wife became so enraged she called up the sheriff. Bolland was arrested again, and his driving permit was put off another year and a half. This made him a little wilder and woolier than before. He spent as much time away from home as possible. In the spring he was all the time hunting muskrats in the creeks, poling a long, flat, double-ended boat of his that had two little runners on the bottom. He claimed he could pole it along on thin ice with his iron-shod pole and when he broke through he just picked up his paddle and went on through the water. Summers he fished a lot, way out on the big lake. One of his favorite adventures was to row himself into the course of the

6

big diesel oil barges that plied the lake, shout to them, grab a line, go aboard and talk and have supper with them while they chugged along north on their inland voyage from New York to Montreal. Then, miles and miles from home, often in the middle of the night, he'd cast off and row all the dark miles back to his home cove. He had a little fish shanty there drawn up on the stones, where he lived most of the time. The hills and the waters were his world, and is there anything wrong with that? It was winter that he liked best, winter when the great lake froze two or three feet deep. He'd take his fish-shanty-on-runners a couple of miles out from shore and there in the blizzards and the sunshine he'd fish for smelt, weeks at a time. Lake Champlain smelt are a famous restaurant delicacy, and sometimes he made two or three dollars a day. His shanty had a little coal stove, a bunk, table, shelves, and was beautifully made like a tiny ship's cabin. About all he came ashore for was to sell his fish and get more coal. Winter was the best time; it was the ideal way for him and his wife to live. Winter nights he'd occasionally come rolling into our kitchen, his red hair on end, his breath strong enough to chin yourself on, a great bulge of tobacco in one cheek. We'd sit by the stove drinking elderberry wine while he told us the secrets of the coves and streams and muskrats and foxes and fish. About midnight he'd stagger out into the cold. I always used to wonder why he wasn't found dead on the ice or in a swamp some morning, but he was one with all that world and is still going strong.

There were more odd fantastic characters per square foot in that township than any other we ever struck. Not all of them were indigenous and harmless, either.

It was way back in the days of prohibition, the great national experiment. Down the Champlain Valley ran the bootlegger routes from Montreal. Across the lake from us about once a week the liquor convoys of fifteen cars all fitted with special tanks used to roar through at night, led by a pilot car. They went through red

7

lights, road blocks or anything else at fifty miles an hour, all police fixed from the Canadian border to Albany.

Sea-going bootleggers landed too at the little cove near us on the Vermont side, a well-protected harbor known as Arnold's Bay in memory of the time when Benedict Arnold beached his boats there and took to the woods to get away from the British who were chasing him down the lake and pounding him with cannon fire. Usually at night, the bootleggers used to nose into the cove in big motorboats, come from the Canadian northern reaches of the lake to be met by trucks. One evening they came to the rendezvous early. At dusk just before the light faded we happened to see silhouetted against the sky a man with a rifle patroling the road. He was one of four, put out on each of the four little dirt cross-roads near Arnold's Bay to bar all traffic while the unloading was in progress. Some farmer called the sheriff at Vergennes that evening and said, "There's bootleggers unloading down here to the lake."

"Thanks," said the sheriff. "Glad you told me. It's a good place to stay away from." And he hung up.

Thus the undermining of a nation's law, its police, its courts and its foundations of government.

The Tanner family, who lived close by the cove, furnished us with many another lurid detail. Once one of the trucks broke down and the bootleggers hid it in the Tanners' barn till it could be fixed. "I wouldn't say nothin'," said one of the bootleggers to Art Tanner that morning and departed. They left no guard, no anything. Arrogance was one of the liquor runners' characteristics. The only people they really feared were hijackers, who had teeth as sharp as their own and maybe sharper.

Art Tanner milked thirty cows and ran a milk truck route as well. He was a gray-haired charming man with a droopy moustache and a watery blue eye. He had a wife and three young daughters who were all as friendly as could be. They taught us to milk and a million things, and seemed glad to have something so strange and

8

curious to think about as ourselves. Art was always sad in a humorous way. With a weary sigh he would pick up a 60-lb. bag of potatoes with one hand and sling it over his shoulder. "Ain't good for much any more," he would murmur, slinging another over the other shoulder and strolling off for the house. Mrs. Tanner was the same only different. They asked us down there to Christmas dinner, and when we arrived she was very apologetic about it, saying, "We ain't got much, but you're welcome to what we have. You'll have to do the best you can." The dinner consisted of roast turkey and roast pork, done to a turn, all you could hold; also five kinds of vegetables from their own supplies, three kinds of pie, two kinds of cake, butternuts, maple sugar, hickory nuts, butter and cream in profuse quantities, and coffee. The Tanners were at that time working the farm on shares, and for the five of them their total net cash income was twenty-six dollars a month. We decided they were the richest poor folks we had even seen. Art was kind of quiet at that meal. He was embarrassed. Early that cold Christmas morning he'd been jouncing along the old rutty road past our house on his milk truck rounds when he got stuck in the mud. I ran out through the new snow and found the hind wheels of his truck sunk to the axles, and he lying in the dirty snow beside it, soaked and freezing, fiddling with something under there. "Christmas morning," he grunted, "and my kids home opening presents." He was so mad the tears were running down his cheeks, and I wished I were somewhere else. "God damn it, I been farmin' forty-five years and look at me," he growled. He banged around with a monkey wrench, his hands full of pliers and mud and snow, time passing, his schedule to keep, Christmas dinner on the fire at home. And then the spasm passed. "Got an axe?" he said, crawling out. I went and got an axe and he cut a slim tree from over by the old pig lot. He jammed the butt end of it under one of his double back wheels, with the other end of the pole sticking out frontwards alongside his front wheel. Then he took a logging chain from the cab, hooked one end to the pole

9

and the other end around the back wheel between its two tires. When he started up the truck, the back wheel served as a winch drum and reeled itself right forward out of the mud along the pole. The butt end of the pole couldn't slip backwards because it was under the truck wheel. Talk about pulling yourself up by your boot straps! Quickly he unhitched his tackle and drove off, arriving home just on the tick for dinner.

The Tanners had a hired man named Ted Norris, a grizzled, short-thick man who seldom spoke, even to children. He was a Harvard graduate who had once been wealthy enough to travel through Europe with a Japanese valet. Inheriting a farm in these parts, he had decided to farm it, but instead of farming he had drunk himself almost to death. During the last of his independent farming days it had been his custom to drive his fine team of black horses eight miles to town to the local inn bar. There as a regular thing he would drink himself senseless. It was well established routine for the bar man to put him into his wagon, bundle him in a robe and start the black team on the road. The horses took him home, not once, but scores of times. Likely they'd be doing it yet except that Ted Norris lost his farm and his team too and hardly made enough now to keep himself in tobacco and overalls. I myself am a Yale man, and so reluctant to record this tragic history.

There were numerous similar swings of the pendulum from wealth to poverty in that town. In the other direction from our house was a beautiful big mansion set up on a knoll overlooking the lake. It had 250 acres of flat fields, and its own beach and boathouse. The horse stable was full of fancy harness rooms and coachmen's quarters and old phaetons and paneled box stalls sheathed better than any house I ever lived in. It was now being worked by a tenant farmer, the old family all split up and gone. Old man Pease who built the place used to telephone to town for a special train whenever he wanted to go the twenty-five miles to Burlington. Then he'd hitch up two Arabs to a gig and gallop them to the station all in a lather. When he had a big job of work he wanted done on the farm he'd go around the countryside telling men to come with their teams on such and such a morning. He paid about ten dollars a day in the days when a dollar was worth something, so they often didn't mind obliging. Frequently enough the wagons would come rolling in in the morning to be met by the foreman who said, "The boss isn't up yet. Just wait around."

"Can't you wake him?"

"Wake Mr. Pease? I should say not!"

So they sat around till noon. They were getting their money anyhow. But Vermonters don't take to pay without work. And toward the end his nature lost all jollity and he became so arbitrary and extreme nobody would work for him at all. He had what the world might call everything—leisure, lands, his house, his horses, his wife, also a trained nurse who was his mistress. And one fine summer night, for all the world like Richard Cory in the poem, he went up to his bedroom and put a bullet through his head.

2

It was one night in March, the wet snowflakes big as blankets hissing up against the old black clapboards outside, when came a knock at the door. We were sitting by the stove as usual. Nobody went by our old house on the lake road at night. The road was drifted up. We were pretty surprised to hear that knocking at nine o'clock at night.

I opened up, and there stood a shortish little dark fellow with the longest nose I ever saw. "How do you do," he said. "Merricks live here?"

"Sure, come in." I saw then that one of his hands was done up in a bloody bandage. "Did you hurt yourself?"

"No, no. That was day before yesterday. I walked out from Vergennes. I wanted to talk to you."

He looked kind of poor, though perky and loquacious as all get out, and Kay soon wormed it out of him that he hadn't had any supper. So we sat him down to some beef stew and beans and a cup of tea, and he began to talk, mostly with his mouth full. He had read my first book and thought it was wonderful. So he decided to come and make our acquaintance. We were pushovers for this, I suppose. He was an odd chap, who had a way of doing whatever came into his head.

It was a couple of hours before he'd half begun to tell his story, and by then it was bedtime and we were asking him to spend the night. He called himself Bill Swami, though that wasn't his real name. He'd been born in India, father was a British expert on Oriental art and his mother a concert dancer, native of India. His father and mother were divorced. His mother had been his father's second wife. His father was now married for the fourth time. Bill had been to school in Switzerland where he had become a terrific skier, but he had never known any home life that would be natural for a child. He was bursting with energy and drive for whatever he wanted, though he wasn't just sure what that was. He was in love with Vermont, particularly the northern region of hills and small lakes up near the Canadian border, and he was living there now, boarding with a farmer in a town called Horseshoe.

"How in Heaven's name did you get way up here?" we asked.

That was a very long story. Now he was making skis. Having formed a partnership with a farmer's son who was a skillful tinkerer, they had put together a little shop and were teaching themselves how to bend and groove and shape maple and birch skis. They had already discovered that birch has a penchant for warping. It was on their new bandsaw that Bill had cut off a finger three days before, which accounted for the bandage. The finger was paining him, and he was still enthusiastic about the new bandsaw—which was typical.

He was still talking when we sent him off to bed. Next day he kept telling us, "You ought to come to Horseshoe to live. Farms are dirt cheap there. I know one by the shore of a lake, abandoned now; an old couple lived there. I'll look into it for you."

That was how we happened to go to Horseshoe in late March, bouncing in and out of the ice ruts in our old Model A Ford. We were by this time looking high and low for a place of our own. And it was pretty hard to find, considering our chronic lack of cash and our utterly unreasonable demands for a perfect farm. It didn't have to be very big, but it had to be the real genuine article, exciting, something to take your breath away, unspoiled, and yet with plenty of wood and water and growing land and possibilities for a living. We used to laugh about the things we wanted, and

13

Kay had it all doped out. "What we really need," she said, "is a place high on a mountaintop, deep in a fertile valley, right beside a sandy beach on the seacoast, with rich loam soil beginning right behind the beach—something on the order of Iowa. We should be miles away from everybody, completely isolated, although marvelous friends are dropping in and out all of the time and the New York Public Library is right next door. We have scads of skiing, interspersed with long periods of hot sun bathing, and although the place doesn't cost anything, it's worth about a million dollars."

"Just a simple little house," I added, "with a fine big cellar, slate roof, two bathrooms and a shop. Also a good barn, fences just right, and enough timber in the woods to pay off the mortgage immediately."

We could run on this way for hours. But, in spite of our impracticality, we had picked up a little sense. We had discovered that it's no good to rent old farmhouses. It had taken us the best part of a year to learn that. And now we were tired of patching other people's roofs and other people's chimneys. The woods were full of old farmhouses in those days, for rent very cheap. The catch was that you had to rebuild them for the owner in order to keep alive in them. We saw now that farming is a very long-time, cumulative procedure, and that getting your fences and fields and buildings to suit you takes years. Often it takes two or three generations to make a satisfactory farm. We weren't getting anywhere on a run-down, rented place, and something had to be done about it. Besides that, it was no fun improving the soil and planting flowers and setting out grape vines for some other fellow.

3

The ruts were very deep, the maples were bare, and the snow still lay deep, though it was melting and making the roads almost intraversable. The old Model A had always had something wrong with its front end. Despite new kingpins and advice from forty garage men it still threw its fore-fenders from side to side with lurches and twists that made it jump in and out of the ruts. A top-heavy crate anyhow, it would now and then do a complete spin on an icy patch and teeter on two wheels for a few moments of suspense while we sat wondering whether it would subside on one of its Tudors or not.

The sky was a dreary gray and the trees were black. The wet snow was no longer good for anything except to get in a persons's way. All in all, a more unpropitious time to go viewing dream real estate would be hard to imagine. But we were pretty hardboiled by this time.

It seemed a faraway land that we were winding into, along crooked roads between countless hills. We bounced up along a road that skirted the east side of a mile-long lake to a black house on a knoll. As always, excitement gripped us while we calculated, explored, plunged through the woods, wondered about the water supply, stuck a jackknife into the sills. We had explored half the northern part of the state looking for a place something like this. Now here was this farm, this lakeside place, with a fine view, 50 acres, 20 tillable, a spring near the house, house badly in need of repair but sound. No running water, no telephone, no electricity, but a home nevertheless. And the complete price was one thousand dollars.

We made the long journey back to our rented acres in a ferment, with the backs of I don't know how many envelopes covered with scrawled designs of fence arrangements, proposed fireplaces and non-existent porches. Kay was busily figuring the rearrangement of the misplanned kitchen while I was running miles of running-water pipe down mythical ditches that never struck ledges. In this country you have to bury a pipe four feet deep if you expect it to continue liquid in winter; but the earth's rock spine is often closer to the surface than four feet.

We were in a frenzy. Trips to St. Johnsbury, meetings with all the relatives who had a share in the place, title searches, vague and disputed boundaries. You can hardly buy an old farm in Vermont without seeing how closely the land is tied up with human destiny and getting all mixed up in the history of several families for the past hundred years. "Our" place had belonged to Uncle Hank and Aunt Mary Baker, who grew so old they couldn't carry on and had to go and live with relatives down in Montpelier. The relatives managed the negotiations, because they were getting the payment in return for their care of Uncle Hank and Aunt Mary. I went to Montpelier and met Aunt Mary, an old woman of 94. Uncle Hank was dead. Aunt Mary seemed to think I was a nice young man, and that was, I believe, the reason why she wished us to have the place. She was so old that, despite a life of poverty, money meant nothing to her now.

The house was jammed solid with hideous furniture, most of which we refused to buy. But we did have to have the three wood-stoves. These we bargained for like mad, and finally I said, "Very well. We'll buy the place for a thousand dollars, but you've got to throw in the stoves or the deal is off." I was ashamed, but I was desperate. The place had been empty for four years, and going down hill for ten. We won.

16

A wooded corner of the property where some tamarack trees grew had uncertain boundaries. I went to the neighboring farmer. He said, "Well, I've always claimed that corner, and me and Uncle Hank rowed about it for years. But it's mostly swamp and a few trees. I claim it, but I'm not going to fight with you about it. It ain't wuth it. That's a one-horse farm. If you like it, buy it." The corner still remains in that state, and neither of us has anything to do with that neglected piece.

I went again to look once more at the property and ran through the woods like a wild man, thinking, This could be ours to live and work in. Uncle Hank had kept one horse and five cows on the place. I was secretly of the opinion that he must have been pretty unenterprising to have had only six head of stock. In one minute I had the fields swarming with cattle and the barn enlarged to hold my bumper crops of feed.

On one of our several preliminary trips we stayed a couple of nights with a farmer and his wife about half a mile south of "our new place." We asked the wife, Mabel Coombs, what she thought of the place.

"Well, it's a good enough little place," she said. "But it's not worth a thousand dollars. Offer them six hundred. And then there's that pond right behind the house. Nobody with a young child like you've got could live right close to that pond. He'd be drowned sure. I'd be worried to death. And likely you'll have more children too." She looked at Kay calculatingly.

We decided that in spite of the liability of the mile-long pond with its lovely coves and islands, we'd take a chance. At last the deal was closed. We were to pay two hundred dollars down and a hundred a year until the thousand was all paid up. I can hardly believe it now. Usually I get the worst of business deals, but that is one I'll always be able to look back on with pride.

Our seventy-mile move from the shores of Lake Champlain to Horseshoe was a rather involved process, like all the rest of it. A milk-truck man from Horseshoe agreed to move us cheap, but he was busy all day and could only manage our move at night. He did not arrive south till midnight, bringing Bill Swami with him to help with the loading. Bureaus, boxes, barrels, tools, and our cow were all loaded into the truck. Our old car was jammed solid too with boxes, bags, food, two young pigs in a sack, our infant son, Bill Swami and half a million other things. We started off ahead, since the truck was slow. At two o'clock in the morning we reached the dark and dilapidated new farm, lit some lanterns and poked around. It looked too old and worn out to be able to stand up much longer, but I knew the cellar wall was solid and the fine eight-by-eight hewn spruce sills were sound as the day they were laid. The Bakers' relative had promised to have the house cleared of furniture, but it was all sitting there as before, completely filling the house. At three o'clock the milk truck with our furniture arrived and backed up to the door. Daisy, our dear old lame Jersey cow, was looking over the tailboard, industriously "daubing up" the furniture behind her—as that fine euphemism has it. I led her off to the dim old barn as rain began to fall in sheets.

There was nowhere to put our stuff except on top of all the other furniture. Tables went upside down onto tables, and chairs on top of those. All that we could leave were narrow aisles here and there about the house. Kim went to bed in his crib completely fenced about with mountains of bureaus and stuff. It was four o'clock when we crawled over three chairs and four tables into our jammed bed in the new house. Rain was dripping through a leak in the roof onto the attic floor, *pat, pat*. We weren't sure whether we liked our new home or not.

In the morning I milked the cow. It was pretty discouraging, looking at the old cobwebby stable ceiling and the whitewash peeling off it. It wasn't a tight ceiling either. Hay stuck through it, and the only way they had kept the stable warm was to store hay on top of it. One wall, the outside wall, was lined with paper to keep out the winter cold, but the paper was all torn now. The plank floor had been worn by the hooves of generations of cows, so that the hard knots stood up and the soft places were grooved. I had no milking stool but resolved to make one. I've always liked making things of wood. Up above the gutter ran a wire about six feet high with a short traveler wire on it and a stiff-springed battery clip. That was for holding tails that switched. There were five good cow stanchions made of maple wood. I wondered whether I'd ever have the five filled. The wood along the inside had been worn satiny by cows' necks. Maple has a wonderful way of wearing smooth, you know, because the grain is so fine. I turned Daisy out to the adjoining pasture while I had a look at the barn floor part and the bays.

It had been wonderfully built, this oblong barn, all framed with first-growth spruce beams, some of them eight inches square and forty feet long. The roof of split cedar shakes had been patched and repatched till the patches wore out. You could see the sky through it in a hundred places. You could see too where rain had been dripping for years on the old spruce timbers. They were still sound as a rock, but they couldn't stay that way forever under such treatment. Way down at the bottom of the walls the foundation stones had fallen away here and there, but the fine old sills bridged such gaps and the barn stood square. Everywhere you looked there was something that needed doing.

I took the milk pail and went across the side yard to the house. The lake right down below our house knoll, and the hills beyond, rolling into the sky—they grew on me minute by minute, and I knew we had an exciting and lovable site for our home, whatever else.

The new stove was drawing beautifully and the breakfast was cooking. A bucket of sparkling spring water was shining on the shelf. Kay was feeding Kim. The little pig was squawking. There was quite a bit of wood in the woodshed. Everything was fine, if we could only get rid of that forest of extra furniture.

First we piled it all in the woodshed and asked the people to come for it. Then we asked them please to come for it. At the end of two weeks we told them we were going to pile it out in the field, rain or shine. Then they came.

It is odd how people reveal themselves by their dwelling places and the accumulated gear of a lifetime. Our house, if it could be called a house, had as its salient quality a certain fortress-against-the-cold aspect. Chinks were crammed with rags and corncobs, all door jams contained shreds of weather stripping, flaps at the bottom, bits of putty and plaster. A lot of the windows were nailed shut. Against the back of the house was a jungle of bushes and little trees to break the northwest wind that swept the lake. So thick were the bushes and tree limbs that a person couldn't move out there. The back door on that side was also nailed fast. Consequently one of my first jobs was to cut out this mess and let the wind go ahead and blow. So much cluttered-up-ness was depressing. The little cellar was all chinked and stuffed up too, and the pipe of the pitcher pump where it ran through the cellar was wrapped in string and rag. The entire atmosphere spoke of forty-below nights.

The cellar was under only one-fourth of the house, but it was snug and a good storage cave for winter supplies. Its floor was solid ledge, "the living rock," and its walls were big mortar-less stone slabs that hadn't budged an inch in eighty years.

The whole outside of the house consisted of age-blackened clapboards, most of which were curling and splitting to pieces. It hadn't had a coat of paint in forty years. The roof needed re-shingling right away.

The upstairs was one great big room like an attic, that ran straight up to the rafters. It had been used as a wood-working shop where they made cedar sap buckets. A workbench stood there, and one corner was piled with buckets, hoops and staves. There was a cobbler's bench too, as though Uncle Hank might have tried his hand at that now and then.

Those old people had a habit of never throwing anything away.

20

There was another little attic above the ell, crammed with clean coffee tins, glass bottles, worn-out implements, broken flails and winnowing-baskets. They kept all their old hats and all their old worn-out shoes in boxes, and there was even a cracked chamber pot which they had tried to mend with cement. The walls were full of India wheat hulls, packed in there by mice. But nobody had raised India wheat in this region for forty years. Under some old straw matting on the floor of a room in the ell were newspapers telling all about the Russo-Japanese War.

4

CHESTER CAME to work at seven A.M. in a buggy drawn by a white horse. He was the father of Swami's ski-making partner. He and his boys and his old white-bearded father had milked thirty or forty cows by this late hour, and the day was well advanced as far as Chester was concerned. Chester's thin shoulders and scrawny whiskers imparted a deceptive quality of fragility.

I had most everything ready for the shingling job that would make our roof tight. I found that the town possessed two fine little waterpower sawmills and one had a shingle machine. Now the sweet-smelling bundles of cedar were piled on the lawn. We had a keg of nails. I had borrowed ladders. It was April and still cold at morning and evening. We were hoping we wouldn't get a rain while a big patch of roof was uncovered.

Chester judged the weather would hold fair, so we cleared off a big section of shingles, shoveling and prying them off with a spade, then pushing them over the edge of the roof in great heaps. By the time we were through, there were heaps of old shingles on the ground banked around the house like snowdrifts, and we had enough kindling to last us for years.

Chester climbed up on the roof and laid on shingles like mad. As we progressed upwards, we perched on a shelf made of a couple of boards supported by several shingle-bundle battens tacked with shingle nails to the roof. "If one brace gives, the others'll hold, probably," said Chester.

In the same breath he claimed he was frightened of heights. "Was up on a long ladder to the eaves of my barn one time, 'bout sixty feet off the ground. The ladder was awful straight on account it could hardly reach. The ladder foot sunk into a soft patch of ground, the ladder spun and I pulled. She commenced to go over backwards. I was climbin' down the rungs as fast as I could go, but I see she was goin' to slam over onto a pile of rocks. Pretty soon I let go and dropped off. Fell about thirty feet. That's how I got my lame leg. But the ladder bruk all to bits on the stun pile."

With Chester on the roof I began a long process of watching and working and learning that lasted for years. Above all, I found that most jobs in building and fixing are no magic, but can be managed by trying and looking and using common sense. Chester, I have often noticed, tries new methods, attempts things he isn't sure of, and if they don't work out, he rips them out and begins again.

In subsequent repair jobs, over a period of years, I found that Chester knew a thousand tricks of construction, tinsmithing, masonry, and carpentry that all save time. If he must fit a board into some odd-shaped place, he lays the board on the place, if he can, squints at it, marks it in place and saws it so. He doesn't like measuring, figuring, splitting sixteenths, plotting angles and all that. Often I have seen him take an old scrap of building paper, fold it into the notches of some queer place, mark its indented creases with the point of a knife, and there he has a pattern for shaping his board, no measuring, no arithmetic at all. Most hard-driven rule-of-thumb men do the same way. They don't like to talk and figure. They say, "Well, let's try it and see how it goes." When roofing, they lay on roof boards and let them stick out any old whichway at the ends, and then when the roof is covered, they snap a chalk line and saw the whole roof edge off even all at once. A beginner, in contrast, will measure every board and try to get the ends even, but they won't be.

23

You may never have thought of it, but one of the fine things about shingles is that every nail is covered. When you are shingling, you work from the bottom to the top, and the upper course laps over the nails of the lower course that you have just put on. The nails would rust out, otherwise, long before the cedar shingles rotted. I don't know how subtle the "subtle chemistry of rain" is, but it's rather sure, like the mills of God that grind exceeding fine.

As soon as we had finished laying on one whole row, or course, Chester got ready and snapped a chalk line with much care the whole length of the roof, to serve as guide for the shingle butts of the next course. It made a pretty blue mark on the brown and gold of the new shingles, six inches up—which meant that two-thirds of their length was covered, and every part of the roof was covered with three thicknesses of cedar. Chester held great gobs of nails in his mouth and fed them out while his hatchet flew in a regular rhythm, two nails to each shingle, breaking joints almost automatically, no fitting, just sizing it up with his eye and planning ahead of time to lay them down right. Now and then his hatchet flashed as he turned it over to split a shingle that didn't lap to suit him. "Wide shingle's no good anyhow. Curls."

Most every morning when we began, the ground was frozen and the roof boards were covered with slippery frost. My hands got so cold sometimes I couldn't hold the nails. I had to go down to the kitchen and warm them and dip them in cold water and warm them again. But Chester seldom followed suit. He scorned such softness, though he was too polite to say so. Now and then it would be too cold to put nails in the mouth; they stuck to the lips. In such case Chester dumped whole handfuls into his carpenter's apron and went on hammering very fast, though not as fast as with the mouth feed. His gnarly fingers that looked so insensitive could manage nails long after mine had turned to icicles. To avoid going down the ladder, I put my hands in on my stomach, Eskimo fashion, to warm them so they'd function. Chester thought that very odd and interesting, but would not do it. There is no New

24

England tradition for that and he thought it rather undignified. I suppose it is.

When we got near the top of the roof slope, Chester started measuring down from the ridge for his chalk-line mark. Heretofore we had been measuring up from the bottom of each course and we might have been going slightly crooked with our rows. That did not matter; he divided the error over three or four courses so that no single row would look askew from the ground. It was all done in a twinkling and looked like nothing, but if I had been alone, my top row would have come out noticeably wrong.

"Why do so many houses here have a wide strip of tin or zinc along the roof at the eaves?" I asked him.

"You'll find out," he said. "Heat from the house melts the snow on the roof, and water runs down to the cold eaves and freezes there. Pretty soon you've got a ridge of ice to back the water up and run it up under your shingles and down the house wall."

When we were putting in flashing around the chimney, he crimped and bent the metal quickly, saying, "There's a chimney over to Bentham I've flashed three times, and it always leaks and always will, I presume. Must be it leaks from the inside.

I could imagine that he had lain awake nights figuring the angles on that chimney, for he is a craftsman and hates to see his work go wrong. He will gladly go and fix a job free if it isn't right. In fact, he insists upon it.

I've been to burned-down barns with him where he looked at the cement floor, uncracked, and said, "I put that in." The countryside, I found, was spotted with jobs he had done, always good ones, always done under difficulties. What was it, I often wondered, that makes a man take such pride in his work. Chester was not robust by any means, and the way he lived, it was a wonder he existed at all. At lunch we found he wouldn't eat this and he wouldn't eat that, never drank milk (though he had forty Holsteins), and was finicky as a spoiled child. He had no teeth and he wouldn't get any, and his clothes hung on him like a scarecrow. I never saw him get angry, even when he banged his thumb on a cold morning. Something very much worse than that had often happened to him; you sensed it in his self restraint and great perspective.

" 'Tain't wuth a Hannah Cook," was one of his favorite expressions of contempt. "It's dirty work, carpenterin'," was another. This rather somber view of his craft had been forced upon him because of the fact that he was forever jacking up the foundations of old barns and putting in new sills. It was a common thing around the town to see Chester poking around some big old barn, prying here and there in a faintly uncertain, ineffectual-looking way, always talking about something else, always with time to talk to the passing mailman or anybody. He hasn't many tools, his overalls are in rags, he hasn't had a shave for two weeks, he charges four dollars a day and apologizes for charging that much. And what happens? Deep under the old 40 x 80 barn Chester is crawling around in the dark, Chester is full of hayseed and cobwebs, Chester is hewing off braces, going here and there with his jacks and axe and crowbars, a stump-puller he's very fond of, and his saws. In about eight days some old lopsided ark of a barn has a new sill, Chester has laid up a new stone wall under it, propped up the cow stable with cedar logs for posts, set the whole thing straight and level, and is gathering up his tools and asking for about thirty-five dollars.

"It's dirty work," he says. He is always having to tear down old buildings for people in order to repair other old buildings, and as he straightens nails and fiddles with old boards, sawing off the rotten ends so they can be used again, he says sadly, "I wish I could build something new once in awhile."

He did build a lot of new things for Mrs. K. Too many. She is one of the wealthy summer folks. He altered her house all to pieces. "She was all the time telling me, 'Now Chester, I want a new window in here, just like that.' So I'd chisel off the clapboards and fit it in fine for her, just like she said, and when I got all done, she'd come and hang her head on one side and look at it and say, 'You know, Chester, I didn't think it would look a bit like that. I think you better move it over five feet.' Crimus, it made me mad. I was puttin' in new windows and doors and pluggin' 'em up again all one summer. I didn't think I could stand it, but I did. One summer she sends me a telegram from France or one of them countries. Says she's found her a painting over there and wants a chimney and mantelpiece so's to make a good place for hanging this picture. She got an architect to make plans for it just so, and mailed them. I built it for her just like she said, and the next summer she come back to look the job over.

" 'My, my,' she says, 'Chester, I didn't think it would look like that.' She was just gettin' ready to tell me to move the chimney, I presume, but I headed her off. I says, 'You can't move the chimney without tearin' down the hull house.'

"I weren't goin' to move no chimney."

We straddled the house ridge, finishing up the last touches, nailing on the saddle boards and moving in opposite directions from our centrally placed chimney. "Now don't back off the end," said Chester. "It's an easy thing to do. On m' Dad's roof on the old house, the shingles below the chimney just about lasted forever. You see these here? They'll never rot where the rain washes lime from the chimney mortar down over 'em. Something about lime makes 'em last. They'll wear thin as paper but never rot. I tried it once, dipping every shingle in a bucket of strong lime water. Makes a roof last ten years longer."

Days on the roof with Chester were always an education. About noon the weather sometimes warmed up and wasn't so bad. It was like being on a lookout tower up there above the lake and the fields and the hills. Off north was a minor range of the Green Mountain foothills meandering across the sky toward Newport and Canada. The lake down below the house was blue and silver, and its islands were dark with fir. Long rock points of glistening gray ran into the water. Beyond our place were the Phillips' fields

27

and Zack's, full of dips and hollows and rollings and hidden stretches that re-emerged further on. South was the Mill Village, and far away, across landscape dotted with farms and fields and dark patches of woods, the steeple of the town church.

I decided I would get Chester to help me with other repairs to house and barn if I ever had the money. Two sides of the house needed new clapboards, among other things. With luck we'd be able to paint the whole place in about three years, white like one of those farmhouses in pictures.

5

IT WAS no use even making lists of the tools and gear we needed; we couldn't buy one tenth of them, only the most inevitable, such as rakes, shovels, scythes, saws, wrecking bar and crowbar. We already possessed axes and most of the simpler carpenter tools. Quite a lot of stuff was already there, lucky for us—a bucksaw, a sledge which I put a new handle into, lots of old chisels and irons. Kay found an immense amount of useful junk in the attic. I made her some bread-baking tins out of sheet tin I got free. We resurrected an old wooden churn and began to make butter, with directions from a government bulletin. In the cellar we found a one-pound butter print mold, all carved—dairy-ish—with leafy bas relief border. The first batch of butter was soft and had an odd taste. Kay proudly gave a pound to Jessie Phillips, our neighbor on the hill. Jessie courageously took the matter in hand. "Your butter is full of sour milk," she said. "Let me show you how to wash it and press it better." And she did, right then and there.

Later on, when we began to get on our feet, we bought a two-gallon glass churn from Sears Roebuck. It had a cast aluminum dasher, not half so sticky as wood. It was geared way up, twenty turns to one, and was a wonder of the age.

As summer came on, one of our greatest joys was to hop out of bed in the morning and run down to the lake for a swim. There it lay, fresh, cool, unrippled, waiting for us, dark and magic, all surrounded with green grass fields and woods. Our high hill and a band of shore-trees cut us off beautifully from the road and we could throw off our pajamas and wade in without suits. What matter if the bottom was a bit rocky and further out there was mud! How many folks were as rich as we, with an estate where they could swim naked in the clear northern water, morning, noon or night, and nobody knew and nobody saw and nobody was going to. I used to feel as the wild ducks must feel, when I was swimming in the morning-cool water those crisp mornings. The system was to light the kitchen wood range on the way to the swim. Then we'd run up the hill and dress by the roaring blaze, the coffee just beginning to perk and scent the kitchen.

What were leaky roofs and cold hands and gray days and rock as compared with such riches of freedom and aloneness.

We worked very hard on the garden that summer, but we had, unfortunately, picked an old garden spot full of witch grass. Witch grass, they say, will thrive quite nicely even if pulled up and hung on the top strand of a fence. It has snaky white roots that nearly always break off when you pull it out. Then the ends start growing again as vigorously as ever. If you break it up in pieces, all the pieces make new plants. They say that buckwheat will crowd it out. For this first summer, however, our only hope in the garden was constant cultivation, which will also kill it after a long, long time. We worked very hard, determined we would lick the stuff, but we had a great many other things to do such as haying and fixing fences and canning. Four days after a good hoeing, the garden would be green with witch grass again. It was only by a steady regime of hoeing, in our little silly cross-rowed garden, that we managed to raise a winter supply of peas and beans, beets, carrots, cabbages and so on. The witch grass got most of our potatoes. Next year, we resolved, we would take a new spot in the field, free from witch grass, and plant in long wide rows so that we could cultivate with a horse, the way all the farmers did. They considered a garden—and a big one—the merest adjunct, something for a woman and child to take care of in their spare time while men went

30

about the more important business of really raising crops. All that the average man did to a garden was to plow, fertilize, harrow it, and later on run through with the horse cultivator a couple of times.

Along the lake road about a third of a mile from us was a low, pretty farmhouse looking across the water to the mountains. Here lived Zack Tyler, an old farmer in his early seventies, who turned out to be an extra good neighbor to us. We had been in our house only a few days when he came driving along in his old buggy and stopped for a chat. "You should have bought my place instead of this," he said. "It's a better farm than you got here."

He spoke the truth. He had seventy-five acres, flatter land than ours, a view across the lake that was equally exciting, and he had quite a good maple sugar bush, as well as some pretty shore line. But we didn't have his price, so that was that.

Zack was getting a mite frail for such heavy work as haying, and sometimes he got discouraged. He couldn't get anyone but a ten-year-old boy to help him with his haying, so he and I combined. He had a team of very old skinny horses with dispositions on the contrary side. No sooner did the going get tough than they stopped, backed to the bottom of the hill, breathed hard, and looked satisfied. The off mare was named Tom and the nigh gelding was named Jerry. Tom was always ahead, Jerry was always behind, and the evener was always uneven. Tom would start the load, and Jerry never got under way until he was about to be dragged.

So we set to haying, Zack and Sammy and I, with numerous stops to grind the mower blades, patch up harness, repair the horse rake shafts, wait out rainy weather, and so on. Sunny days it was hard, heavy work, of course, the barn full of chaff and devil's paint brush seed to make you sneeze, hayseed down your neck, the sun burning and the work going on and on. Neither of us had hay-loaders in our barns, so we had to pitch off the hay as well as pitch it on. Zack got kind of blue around the gills sometimes. Sammy and I pitched on the tumbles as the wagon slowly creaked between the haycocks. Zack was on the wagon, making the load, because that took the most skill and was slightly less wearing. Zack tried to hold up his end, but the pitching off in the barn took his wind and bothered his heart. He had to stretch out flat and gasp sometimes, while we went and got cool water from the spring and put pads on his forehead and wrists. Then he'd sit up and blink, hang a smile on his cheery old face, wipe off his steamy glasses and say, "Well, boys, here we go. What're we waitin' for." While the wagon rattled out to the field he let Sammy drive, and sat swinging his legs, singing in a cracked tenor a sentimental love ballad called "Over the Garden Wall," or another heart-rending lament called "When I Can Have My Title Free and Clear," which dealt with mortgage payments and the love of a good woman.

One afternoon all up and down the field of haycocks he was damning the big milk handlers who buy his milk and give him "nothing," damning the markets, damning the witch grass and the dry weather, damning the hailstorm that lodged his oats, damning the milk inspectors who came around and demanded improvements to the milkhouse and the stable and the sanitary arrangements. "They can take my milk or not. I'd lose less if they didn't. I ain't a-goin' to ruin myself to make them rich. Forty year I been at this, workin' from five in the morning till seven at night, and what did I ever get out of it! Hey?"

We drove into his barn, which was only about a quarter full of hay, and he had but two more loads to bring in from his run-out fields. He was keeping only four cows on a farm that used to feed ten. As I pitched off and he mowed away, his old face streaked with dirt, his glasses steamed up, he shouted: "B'God, I seen the time when this barn was plumb jammed full till you couldn't see the ridgepole—and right off this farm. The shed was full and I sold twenty-five dollars worth standing too."

"That so?"

32

He leaned on his fork. "Yes, sir! How many years you think it would take me to plow the fields and seed 'em down and bring this farm back till I could fill this barn with hay and have a stack outside to boot? Hey?"

"Oh, about a thousand," I said.

"No, sir! Three. Three years!" He stood there in the mow, leaning on his fork handle, an old man, with a look on his face like the picture of Balboa discovering the Pacific.

6

NEITHER OUR NEIGHBORS, relatives nor our former friends understood the simplicity of our simple lives. We believed in simplicity. We loved our spring full of water in the hollow, and our woods full of trees and our blue lake and our green grass field. To see our own cow cropping our own grass—it was something very fine to us. For a stranger I suppose it would be nothing much; just a black shack and one lame cow in a thin field. They might have said to themselves, "How can people live like that."

It was our idea that it might be possible to go directly after the things you want. We wanted to write and farm, so we wrote and farmed. I never thought it sad that the old fences were falling down. I thought it was wonderful our woods were full of cedars for new fence posts, and that I could scrape together money for a little new wire now and then.

It is a quiet evening and I have been lying in the alders watching wild ducks on the lake. There is a very special wildness about autumn evenings such as this, cool and crisp and still as a broken clock that might start any minute. It is the stillness, perhaps, that makes the wooded points, the brook mouth here, the hills, the mirror lake, the first stars, one vast enthralling work of art. I wonder for how many centuries on evenings like this the wild ducks have swept out of the sky and circled in with that heart-rending curve of speed to this very cove.

There is no motion on the water except their shining wakes. Sometimes one flutters a wing. They dive, all of them, and the ripples widen out and gentle. In the center of the growing circles the water turns to glass again as though they had vanished forever. But, fifteen or twenty yards on, they break water, churning like little tugboats. They dart and dive as though they were playing tag, wheeling and twisting with madly beating feet; they rush half flying over the water, their wings a-whistle with the duck sound, breasts high, six miniature seaplanes, "up on the step." Their throbbing wings beat faster, and then, voluptuously belittling their power to hop steep into the air, they merely skim the cove, inches above their reflections. For minutes they skim, so close the unbroken surface trembles with their passing, until they tire of it and come in again on a wide, racing curve to meet the water with trailing feet, and splash and breast up a surge. They peck and feed and dive and bob, and now and then one of them tears a white gash in the black water.

It is suppertime for me too, and I go home. A cow bell is tinkling on a hill across the lake.

The autumn wind roars through the maple tops, ripping the foliage to shreds, shouldering the trees. It is big and careless and bluff and hurts a little already, and doesn't care. It makes me think, not just of the coming long winter, but of the old philosophies of joy and pain, while the tree limbs writhe and roar and the leaves fly down by the thousands. Walking the little old dirt roads at this time of year, you come round a bend and wonder where the road lies, it is so deep under drifts of red and yellow leaves.

Along about this season the old folks say in the little white farmhouses beside the big red barns, "I dread the winter, I do. I dread the winter." They roll it over and over on their tongues, between their store teeth, having no other joy than this old familiar yearly anticipatory dread, which they have lived with so long

35

they enjoy it. And when they get very *very* old, they talk about not living to see the spring, and that sometimes keeps them going in fine style till May and June and the balmy days of lilacs, strong and sweet in the northern sunshine.

The north wind roaring down in October is cruel and cold and reminds you again—as the sea has a way of doing—that nature does not care for man. And somehow that makes the red and yellow leaves and the blue, deceptive noons all the sweeter and more precious because living is so dangerous and so short and can be so bitter. The fall, cold, shouldering wind makes me think of fishing skippers who will tell you that a thirty-mile winter wind has twice the weight and solidity of a thirty m.p.h. summer wind. They take a reef in winter for the same wind they would laugh at in summer.

And now we take our reefs. We check our storm windows and cabbages and all the old husbandry ways. To be happy in this country you must be like the Eskimos and welcome the snow. We are glad of the frozen-lake roadways and the filled-in wood roads, the hardened swamp, the skiing, the wood and the fires and the long nights for sleeping.

7

ALTHOUGH the house was roomy, so little of it was heatable and habitable in winter that we were distinctly cramped. In fact, all that was warm was the kitchen, living room, and a bedroom off the living room. Kim's bedroom was in the wing, adjoining the tiny living room and stove. At night when we went to bed, we opened his door so he got some warmth. In spite of this, a patch of water spilled on his floor in December stayed there as ice till March.

Well, it's always so with settlers. If you can get through the first year, you'll probably survive. No promises, you know.

The wood was green. I was always worried about the chimney and the mortar out of it. I pointed it up—anyone can fool around with small jobs of cement, I soon found out. I bought new stovepipes immediately, as I discovered part of one elbow burned out in pinholes.

The barn was very cold for Daisy, patched with building paper, heaps of straw here and there. She had no bedding except the big stacks of maple leaves we had gathered in the woods before snow came. I had to hang up a curtain at the end of the little cowstable, dividing off the horse stalls, or she would have frozen. Even so, manure in the new wooden gutter I had put in froze solid to the boards in the morning. Snow drifted in through the holes in the upper side walls, but not enough to hurt much. The roof leaked whenever there was a thaw.

Kay was wrestling with that kitchen, no room for anything, shelves covered with dust. The wind roared across the lake with the strength of some ancient wild horse legend, making the old black house rock and groan. But it was solid. Our fine new stoves functioned beautifully, their silver trim gleaming cosily. The kitchen range turned out to be a good baker, and we could throw some bread slices into the oven at breakfast and make the finest golden toast in about two minutes. Our heater-stove in the parlor was a squarish box with a door in one end and a big lid that opened on top. In through that top lid at bedtime we could drop a big knotty chunk, turn the damper, and in the morning the stove was full of great blue and gold coals which we stirred to a blaze.

I cannot say why we loved it still. We were the settler people and no mistake. We made what we had. It was the land around us that made us love it, our green woods, our white lake, our barn, our house, our wood to burn, our own lives for our own selves. We knew we could make it cosy and homelike eventually, though it would take us years. It had space, it had beauty, it had the materials, the soil and wood and water for enabling us to make a living for ourselves and for our children. When everything got too much for us indoors, we put on our mittens and moccasins and parkas, twisted on our snowshoes and went for an afternoon through the sugar woods and over the white and lonely hills, and we knew we were doing right and that everything was okay. Who can explain what it is that makes people function? I always felt good that I was working for myself at something I knew was good, and that was recompense for all the inconveniences and poverty and tribulations. In the late winter the deep snow became a blessing. It drifted in around our old house covering the sills, covering half the back windows, keeping the wind out and making us warmer in the 30-below nights of February than we had been in the zero times of bare November. At night after milking in the barn, I would kick some snow against the cowbarn door and know that Daisy would be warmer thanks to the deep banked drifts.

Some afternoons when it was too wet to work in the woods, Zack dropped over for a visit. One sloppy, sleety afternoon we sat by the stove, talking of this and that, and came around to the subject of cities and how big they are. I agreed with Zack that most of them are too big. Mayor LaGuardia said New York City is altogether too big, and he ought to know. Zack was telling me he was up to Sherbrooke, Canada, once.

"That Sherbrooke is a big place I want to tell you. You can get lost in it easy. There's places where the buildings are so thick and high the sun never strikes. I was up there one time and nightfall come on and I was caught there with no way to get home. I had to spend the night in a hotel. Slept *seven storeys up!*"

He puffed his pipe. "Slept real well, too."

The region was full of heartening eccentrics, of course, and it took a long time to know and appreciate them. Old Doc Hester, before he died, was one of the strong foundations of East Totenboro. He was the real old country doctor, battling the elements in a buggy. He was a great fisherman too, and knew all the mountain roads and brooks from here to Jay Peak. On a sick call he would go anywhere, night or day, in any weather. If the snow was drifted too deep for his horse to wallow through, he'd put up his rig at the nearest house and snowshoe the rest of the way. Whether people could pay him or not made no difference. If they were very poor he sometimes told them not to worry about it. In consequence he was pretty poor himself. But toward the latter part of his life he took a flyer in stocks, and, strange to say, cleaned up. His cousin sums it up very aptly: "You see, old Doc Hester, he never got any of the money he earnt, and he never earnt any of the money he got. And here's another funny thing. Hester didn't care whether you paid him or not so long as you got well. Most new

39

doctors are quite the other way around. They don't care whether you get well or not so long as they get paid."

Old Newt Halloway sits up straight in his battered car and drives it as he would a horse. When he has a puncture, it's generally in the nigh or the off fore tire, because he keeps the best shoes on the hinder wheels. He sells Larkin spices, and pins and cow spray. He buys muskrat and mink and fox skins, also skunk and coon. He buys bull calves, he buys hides, he buys most any old thing and pays what he thinks is right. But if down at the tannery he happens to get more for a calf hide than he figured, you'll see white-haired old Newt Halloway driving back in his loppy old car to the farmer to say in his shy, apologetic way, "Here's thirty-five cents more. I got a better price than what I thought for."

Newt has a cedar-still and he makes cedar oil at seasons when there isn't anything else to do. Last year Newt paid the town fifty dollars—it was in the town report, the proudest statement in that pertinent little contemporary history book—for what do you suppose? For fifty dollars worth of food supplies which the poormaster granted ten years ago to Newt's now-deceased brother.

Old Newt Halloway, the raggedy old man, vestigial tinker, last remaining—he keeps his honor bright with cedar oil. There are men on the town who live better than Newt. But he wouldn't trade places with them.

A man came up to help me cut ice today. He has a wooden leg which makes him limp badly. Lately he has been cutting wood. He is "on the town," a fellow who works very hard, but cannot get a start or a place of his own. He works much harder than I do, but he cannot make a living.

It was ten below on the lake where we were sawing out blocks with hand ice saws. His saw he made out of an old drag-saw, and it is better than my bought one. He had no mittens, just a pair of heavy leather gloves, the bare leather with no linings. And they were worn out. The palm of one hand was all exposed, and from the other glove two fingers stuck out. He worked all afternoon, and would no more think of going up to the house to get warm than of flying over the moon. When the sun went down, the temperature went down with it. The lake commenced to boom, and the hills grew black. About dark he limped along toward home.

It has often seemed to me that the men who are most exposed to cold have as a general rule the poorest clothing, that men who most need fine, strong modern tools that our age so boasts of cannot have them, that the men who do most work have least food. Who has the best wagon? It is usually a man who dallies in horse shows. The farmer has an old half-rotten thing that was worn out years ago. Which woman's kitchen has all the labor-saving devices? Is it the woman who must cook for twelve threshers? No sir, it is a spinster dame who has three maids and a cat. It is the same with windproof clothing, fur hoods, goat's-wool stockings and all the rest. They are for skiers who go out a couple of weekends a year. The man who works out of doors every day all winter never heard of such things. His clothes are made of cotton of the cheapest kind. The people who most need electric water pumps, washing machines, sawrigs, oil burners, sewing machines and all the rest, do not have them. The old cars, the aged trucks, the leaky boats with uncertain motors, the rusty ships, the undernourished men—they carry most of the world's burdens. Oh well, it has always been so and it will always be so so. Pegleg might be worse off if he were a successful Junior Executive with a starched collar and an ulcer.

It is bright moonlight now, glittering on the frosty crust and on icy patches in the road; cold as Greenland's icy mountains and perfectly still except for the lake booming and cracking as it tightens.

Pegleg will be home, sawing tomorrow's firewood with a bucksaw. He will be glad of the moonlight because it saves him burning oil in his lantern.

8

DAYS, MONTHS and years went by so fast at our farm we could hardy keep track of them. We sold our Model A, which had always been a nuisance and could seldom go by a garage without stopping. To take its place we acquired a secondhand Buick that was a daisy. It was a buff-colored sport touring Master Six. It was nine years old when we bought it for thirty dollars, and it was the joy of our hearts. It was long and heavy and huge, with big high wheels and a frame almost the size of a railroad rail. It never bounced; it lunged and swayed. It had big pockets in the doors, and beside the driver a tool pocket full of wrenches and stuff. It had a cloth top, curtains, a thermometer surmounting the chromium radiator cap, two-wheel brakes, and real leather cushions made of the finest black cowhide. It had a walnut steering wheel. There was nothing synthetic about it from stem to stern.

It was the swaying powerful motion of it that intrigued me. It seemed to weave and bend over the road humps, the sound of its hum in second gear was enough to carry your soul away, and when, by careful nursing on a long straight stretch, you were able to get her up to fifty-five, you felt as though you were creaming through the countryside in a Pullman. It was wide open too. The sides hit you at about the belt, and you could really see what was going on. Mostly we had the top down. It was so big the driver could stretch his legs right out straight. Cars weren't low and wide in those days; they were high and narrow, and this one was extra high and narrow. Kay had to have two cushions behind her to manipulate the pedals. It steered a little like a truck. And though it was nine years old, it was as good as the day it was made. Everything about it was a joy to the heart—except the gas bill.

It had huge hard tires. On account of its high wheels there never was such a car for mud and snow. We always carried a logging chain in the back, and we pulled new low shiny jobs out of ditches, mudholes and snowdrifts by the dozens. We'd come to a road in the spring, blocked by a couple of cars stuck, men prying with fence rails, digging, cursing. We'd turn around, hook our logging chain to them and out they'd come, like Venus rising from the sea. Then we'd plow through nonchalantly ourselves, without a quiver. When she settled down till she was sliding on her running boards and her back wheels were sunk in solid, she could draw like a prize team of oxen. It gave us huge joy. We used to go over the pass to a spot called Eden via a road that at the top was nothing but a brook bed full of stone step waterfalls. Passengers sometimes had to get out and be seasick on the grass, but the big buff Master Six Sport Touring never turned a hair.

Never was such a car. It was an individual, a member of the family. It was the only car like it in this whole section of Vermont, and everywhere we went, people waved to us, recognizing the old yellow Buick, feeling the same friendliness for its individual powerful bulk as we did, I guess. Once in the White Mountains a car approached that was its twin brother. My mouth and its driver's mouth fell open. Without thinking we both jammed on the brakes and pulled up side by side. "Where'd you get it?" he beamed.

"Oh, aren't they something," I replied.

He was from Boston, had had his four-wheeled beauty willed to him by a brother. "And I wouldn't trade it for a house and lot."

"Do you use much gas?"

"Oh well, now—now, not much, considering the fun I have."

We compared mileage, tires, upholstery, paint. His had been 150,000 miles. Mine had been to Georgia three times, twice to

Mexico, and to California and back, I knew, before the speedometer broke.

A car was coming, and we were blocking the road. "So long, brother," he said, holding out his hand. "Keep up the good work." And so we parted, those beautiful heavy gears, low, and second, and high, singing as we accelerated. It was quite a sentimental encounter.

We could fill the back seat with grain bags. Inside the front fenders were snug spots for bags of mash too, with another inside the front bumper. It had springs like the rest of it, strong as Sampson, and none of this powder-puffy, feather-beddy feeling. We could load in eight people, 400 pounds of grain, a few tools, and never hit the wheels. It was rare that anything on it wore out or went to pieces, though I did once find the battery box corroded to rusty flakes, and the battery hanging by the cables, just clearing the road.

In winter it was a devil to start. Putting a pan of coals under the transmission sometimes helped, though that was dangerous in the hay barn. We used to keep the car some winters at the Mill Village, half a mile away, where we rented a garage shed beside the plowed road. We'd walk down to the Mill Village, try to start her, and we wouldn't even be able to turn her over in that thirty-below temperature. You could mesh the crank and then jump up and down on it. The crank wouldn't budge. Then we'd walk back home again. Very good exercise.

One evening there was a good movie on at Morrisville, eighteen miles away. It was in January. We read of it in the local paper. The movie was "Eskimo," from the book by Peter Freuchen, and he himself was playing the part of the fur trader in the movie. We were enormously interested in Freuchen, with his great red beard and flamboyant personality. We considered him one of the world's great arctic travelers and thought the book "Eskimo" a minor masterpiece, one of those rare combinations of authenticity and storytelling drama. Freuchen, a Dane, had formerly operated the most northerly trading post in the world. He had an Eskimo wife

44

and spoke Eskimo himself. We had heard that once when he was visiting in America, Mrs. Rockwell Kent expressed a great admiration for his red beard. Freuchen took a pair of shears, hacked off a large chunk of it and presented it to her.

Well, we spent the day getting the old Buick warmed up and going. Jessie Phillips came down to stay with Kim in the evening. It was a regular arctic night, with deep snow and bright stars, so we decided to put the top down. We had a wonderful foot-rigging consisting of sheepskin slippers inside arctics which we wore most everywhere to keep our feet from freezing. We'd go to Montpelier and everywhere with these bedroom slippers hidden inside our arctics, and nobody knew the difference. We had fur mittens, woolen underwear, fur coats, and a huge robe.

The snow was squeaking, and off we roared, just the tips of our noses showing to the icy wind as we rolled down the curving track of the plowed-out road to Morrisville. The lights on the snow, the stars glowing—it was an adventure for us, because we hadn't been anywhere in a long long time. I guess the thermometer was about 25 below.

The movie was wonderful, but when we came out, a heavy snow was falling. The car seats and tonneau were as full of snow as a basket. I tried to start her, and she wouldn't register at all. No lights, no starter, no horn, no anything. It was about eleven o'clock in the little town, and the street was by this time deserted. I did find a man who told me of a garage mechanic nearby. It was a two-family house with an outside stairway to the garage man's upper apartment. He was sitting cosily by a stove with his shoes off, and he said, "It ain't a Ford is it?"

"No it's a Buick."

"Okay. So long as it ain't a Ford. I always hate to shut myself up inside of one. I don't fix 'em." Whereupon he put on his shoes and coat and tramped down the stairs as though it were the most natural thing in the world to be rousted out at eleven o'clock on a winter night.

He took her in with a glance. "Oh, a big old Buick, eh. No ignition. Hm." He stuck his hand in under the dashboard, wiggled some wires, and said, "Now try her."

Off she went, like a clock. "Sure," he said. "Those old Buicks, they got an odd connection in there. They do it all the time." He took his flashlight, and together we stood on our heads under the dashboard while he showed me the thing. He wiggled it with his bare hand. "There. You see?"

We crawled out and flapped our arms.

"Gosh," I said, "we can't thank you enough. Here's a couple of dollars for getting you out at this time of night. Will that be all right?"

"Oh, that's nothing. I don't want any money," he said, and he walked off with his hands in his pockets. It was too good to be true, and I'd suspect that he is a figment of my imagination if it weren't that he has fixed cars dozens of times for us since then. When he really gets to concentrating on an engine noise with a stethescope, I never saw a mechanic like him.

So we swept out the snow, climbed aboard, and rolled home, past all the dark farmhouses, the falling snow dancing in the headlights, the drifts deepening, up the hills, rounds the bends, deep in the cold night, deep in the stars, deep in the fur. Jessie was asleep on the couch in the living room, the stove purring, warm as a caress, the room deliciously hot. I walked up the hill with her, carrying a lantern because she is afraid of bobcats and claimed to have heard one screech the night before.

9

ONE OF OUR FAVORITE personalities in these parts is the lady at Robbins' Hardware store, in Bentham Bend.

I go in to buy a water pitcher. It's an event, both for me and for Miss Robbins, though neither of us can share the other's emotional tempest.

"Have you any water pitchers?" I say.

"I *think* so," she replies, "—*if* I can *find* them." Things fall, things slide with a gritty wound. She reaches high, she gropes low. "Well, here's some."

"Oh yes," I say. "They look pretty good."

"They don't *pour* very well."

"But this light aluminum is quite soft. I could probably bend the lip so it would pour all right."

"Maybe you could," she says, brightening, nodding her head sagely. She hadn't known I was such an enterprising fellow. She looks me over interestedly, speculating whether I am smart enough to cope with such a refractory water pitcher as this one—and she compliments me, saying, "I presume you could, yes."

Well, I buy the pitcher, and she takes it from me lingeringly, questioningly, on the alert for a sudden about-face, smiling gently to put me at my ease in case I want to change my mind. But I am adamant, and I buy it.

"Oh," I say. "Have you any Bordeaux mixture? That makes pretty good spray dope for bugs on cabbages, doesn't it?"

47

"Hm-m. Well, I never used it myself—on anything. But we've some boxes of it somewheres, I think. AL-BERT! What was it Pa used to put on the cabbages for them green worms?"

A wizened-up, white-haired fellow who looks old enough to be her great grandfather, creeps out from the shadow of stoves, wheelbarrows and trash at the back of the store. "Salt," he croaks.

"Salt! that's it. I remember." Miss Robbins beams happily at the memory. "Table salt, cattle salt, any kind of salt. Yes, probably you've got some home." She bobs about, wiggling her shoulders discreetly, relieved to have the cabbage situation cleared up for me.

"I don't believe salt really kills the bugs very thoroughly," I say. "It may be all right after the cabbages get pretty big and you don't like to put poison on them, but these are little plants I'm talking about, and the worms are slaughtering them. Could I see the Bordeaux?"

"Very well." She goes off rummaging, piqued now that I am not satisfied with her revered father's methods. It is a distinct slight, not only upon him but the excellence of the cabbages he raised. She gets quite brisk, she is quite offended.

By George, in her anger if she doesn't find the stuff—a dozen one-pound boxes of it down behind a hopper full of carriage bolts, slightly rusted.

In a silence fraught with antagonism she sets a box before me on the counter. After all, let no one say that she has been remiss in fulfilling her duties to a customer, no matter how outrageous his whims. I blow the dust off and read the directions, she eyeing me the while, coldly, her head turned aside and her lids half lowered.

"I believe I'll take it," I say. "How much is it?"

Surprise, shock, incredulity succeed one another upon her angular face. She bows her head, lowers her eyes to the floor with a species of timidity—and shame that it is so much. Then summoning all her forces she lifts up one eye very wide, cocks

48

her head and groans an apologetic question, "It's seventy-five cents . . . ?"

So I buy the Bordeaux mixture too.

"Thank you," she says primly.

"Thank *you*," say I. "You know, this is my favorite store in all the world. For after all, what is life without contrast."

She looks confused. She wonders if I'm sane. But she is equal to the emergency. "We *try*," she says, "to oblige."

Knock, knock at the door on a cold rainy day. It was an old man in an ancient car, selling maple syrup. His hair was gray and his whiskers long. He had a strangely vague way about him. He had brought with him a teaspoon and an open can, which he insisted that I sample. It was delicious. He called it "the honey" as distinguished from the sugar, which he was also peddling in 25-lb. pails. He said business wasn't very good, most everybody had their own. He cast his eye around the place. "You haven't got any old auto tires, have you?" It seemed he burned them in the furnace of his evaporator and they made a hotter fire even than coal. I said I hadn't, but that I'd buy a gallon of syrup. He stood and dripped while I went to get the change.

I didn't know at the time that he was the famous Old Man Bushwell. Our neighbor, Lane Kent, who lived beyond the Phillips, told us, "Why, he's so dirty, they say he strains his syrup through a leaky rubber boot. He's pretty dirty, for a fact. He lives all alone now, had a married couple living at his place but he turned them out. The woman was neat and tidy and kept things clean. He couldn't stand it. He's used to havin' the hens run in and out the kitchen, and he most always has a calf or two in the woodshed near his door. The turkeys roost in the house too if they want to. He can't abide women, nor funerals either. He used to live out on the main road, and if ever a hearse went by, he ran into the house and stood with his back against the door. I get on well enough with him. I used to take him to town before he got a car.

49

I'll tell you, though, once he asked me to get him some groceries. Well, when I got back, I drove into the dooryard and walked up the steps. Bushwell come to the door and said he'd take the bundles.

" 'That's all right,' I said. 'I'll bring 'em in. I got 'em in my arms.'

"Bushwell didn't want to, but he stepped back out of the way. 'Come kind of careful, Lane,' he says. 'My old sow's in here farrowin', and she's havin' an *awful* time.' "

All unaware of this (the syrup never hurt us) I returned to Old Man Bushwell with the change, and went out to the road with him. "Say," he said, as he got into his car, "you haven't got any old auto tires, have you?" His eyes kind of wandered down onto the ground and he drove away. The trees were bare and black, and the clouds hung low. I had an idea the wind would whisk him and his car into the sky like a witch on a broomstick, while he was grinding along the dirt road toward the woods.

Lo and behold if a school teacher and his wife didn't buy a 200-acre farm on the upper lake three miles beyond us and start a summer camp. First thing you know they had twenty cabins, six saddle horses, three cars, nine boats and fifty youngsters up there. They were fine people, and we all came to be good friends. One of my summer jobs after that was being an ex-officio counselor at the camp, particularly on trips. The director and his wife didn't know much at first about the rivers and lakes roundabout, so I was "commodore" of their canoe trips. I had two girl paddlers and reclined amidships on cushions while the little fleet slid north along beautiful Lake Memphremagog. My two girls about broke their backs because it was a matter of pride with them to keep the Commodore well ahead of the other canoes. I felt rather sorry for them, but they were so proud that my sorrow gradually lessened. Also, we had rainy days, and reclining in two inches of water will dampen anybody's spirit. We camped on the beaches and islands and points, and at night we had campfires while the wavelets lapped in the darkness. The cooks rotated, and each crew had been trained during many long preparatory weeks to build his fire, make his griddle cakes, wash his dishes, or whatnot. It was a fine system, except that just about the time the boy or girl cook began to acquire the first glimmerings of competence in the difficult art of cooking on the trail, she was rotated, and on came Patsy DePeyster, whose mother had been divorced five times and was negotiating a sixth. Most everybody learned to pack about his person a box of raisins and a bar of chocolate, so that if the supper didn't come off till ten o'clock, the suffering was not too acute. The kids had to learn, and they learned, by the best way there is— experience. We had some bad thunderstorms that could swamp a loaded canoe if we didn't see them coming far ahead and find shelter in a bay. Thus they learned something about weather also. In our travels we pretty well plastered the shores of Lake Memphremagog with left-behind and forgotten flashlights, kodaks, wrist watches, jackknives, compasses, bar pins, junk jewelry, bathing suits, packs of cards, diary books, socks, sweaters, and an occasional shoe, but we never lost a camper, and that was the main thing.

A man they hired at the camp to help build up the place was Ethan Cutler, who lives in the little town of Albany nearby and is as solid as his name. He was a great find for them, full of tales of local lore, an ardent hunter knowing all the trails around, and he was the ingenious Yankee when it came to working in wood or metal. He had a wood lathe and a metal lathe at home and a collection of tools that a two-horse wagon could hardly carry. He had taught himself all sorts of things about the geometry of carpentering and the expansion of metals. He built boats that didn't leak, and would set up a cabin all alone in one week, levering timbers you'd suppose three men couldn't handle. He and the director did the plumbing for the place and set up the hydraulic ram. Ethan managed the lumbering job when the camp got out its own timber for building. The camp children took to him immediately, and he made pretty good carpenters out of some of the apartment-house small fry from Manhattan.

One day Ethan and the camp director and I were walking up the crazy valleys in the folds of Albany Mountain. Ethan was showing us one of the crooked passes over to the valley beyond. There were some old cellar holes back in there, and about seven miles in, up along a beautiful brook with a waterfall, we came to a clearing known as the old Shute place. Ethan said, "Old Jacob Shute married a girl seventeen years old down to Albany and brought her back up here. She never went down to town for eleven years, and in that time she had ten children. Along toward the end of the eleventh year she calculated she'd go down to Albany for a visit. She walked down to town and she stayed there. Old Jacob never got 'er back."

It was autumn and the sod was wet and the leaves were falling. We were awakened by a roaring out on the front lawn. It was Lyman Phillips' black bull pawing the turf and bellowing as though he meant to beat a hole in the house. His horns were very sharp and his eyes were wicked. I happened to know his age very well because I had recently been reading of bull fatalities in Pennsylvania. In my book it said you can't trust a bull over two years old, because he's certain to turn savage at some time or other when you least expect it. This bull was two-and-a-half years old.

Chester's hired man had been telling me about bulls, too. A big one turned on him once in a barnyard, quick as a cat, and threw up a horn point that caught him between the pants and the belt. That's how close it was. The bull dangled him by the belt and tossed him ten feet in the air. The fellow was near the fence when he fell, and, though groggy, had presence of mind enough to roll under the bars before the bull could mash him with two bone-crushing front hoofs.

So this was what had come over Lyman's bull! I had to give up studying him through the parlor window because it made the black beast so mad. A pitchfork was what we needed. But our pitchforks were in the barn.

I lit the fire and put the coffee on, hoping that somebody from Lyman's would come down and do something with this irrational engine of destruction. Of course, it's a well-known fact that the simple life on a farm is a constant series of emergencies. The cows are in the corn, the roof's afire, the horses are running away, the well is dry, the sheep are sick, and a thunderstorm is about to drench the thrice-tumbled haycocks in the field. At first it's all very wearing, but by and by you don't mind very much and learn to take the emergencies in your stride. However, if there's anything I hate, it's bullfighting before breakfast.

Nobody came, and the bull continued tearing things up out front. It was plainly up to me to lift this siege. Suppose our child had been playing around outside when the monster came along? The Phillips should never have let him get loose in the first place. But how to get out of the house to summon them?

I sneaked out the back door and way down the back hill where the bull couldn't see me, then circled round, with the barn between me and him, and edged in the barn door straight to a good, sharp, three-tined pitchfork. With this in my hand I felt better as I slid out of the barn again and around a clump of bushes for the road. The bull hadn't seen me, which suited me just as well, and so I legged it up the hill to Phillips'.

Lyman and his son, Bob, were in the barn milking. "Your bull's loose," I shouted, "and he's tearing the place to pieces down at my house."

Lyman leaned back on his milking stool and said, "That so?" He thought a minute, and then he said, "Robert, go down and see to that bull." He tipped forward on his stool and went to milking again.

53

Bob was a pink-cheeked cherub fifteen years old, with freckles and a most engaging smile.

Bob went out to the barn floor and picked up a flail of ash wood. It consisted of a four-foot handle with a thong in the end linking it to another wooden piece about three feet long--sort of a hinged club which they used for threshing dried beans. As we skinned down the hill, I said to Bob, "What will you do? We'd better kind of plan, eh?"

"You'll see," he said. He marched straight up to the bull and fetched him a clip on the head with the flail. Then he walked around behind and walloped the bull on the rump, saying, "Hi yar! get along home, stupid!" The bull tucked his tail down and scampered for the Phillips' with a sidewise, crestfallen gait that would have been quite funny if it hadn't been so unexpected.

"Gosh, Bob, thanks," I said.

" 'Tain't anything," he replied. "He's only a young one." He folded up his flail, cocked it over his shoulder, and walked along home after the bull.

I watched him go and thought, now there's a country kid for you. As a little tyke he plays with stones and curious rocks, falls into brooks and crawls out again, whittles blocks of wood into boats, chops kindling with a 3-lb. axe, fires the furnace at sugaring, builds himself shacks in the woods, explores, gets lost, finds a way home again, tames a pet crow, helps with the butchering, milks night and morning, breaks colts, handles on a halter fractious heifers ten times as strong as he is, endures the scratch of berry bushes and bite of flies. He looks at a stranger coolly, and at fourteen answers as a man would.

Mornings when I got up very early in the dark, I'd often see Bob's lantern swinging along the far shore of the lake. He was tending his trapline and had already been round the nearer shores of the upper lake and down the alder-choked brook that connects the two. I could picture him baring his arm and reaching down into the cold water under an old tree root by the brook rapid,

54

then drying his arm on his pants. He had a mink trap there. Now and then he got a fox or a muskrat, and with these he bought his mittens and other winter clothes, as so many farm boys do. At 8:20 A.M. he trudged by on the road for school three miles away, having milked seven or eight cows and eaten breakfast. He smiled and waved if he saw anybody, and sometimes on the way home he dropped in to say hello if he could spare the time.

An oldish man came trailing along the road at dark one night, stopped at our house and said he could not walk any farther. He gave us his name, and proved to be the uncle of a farmer whom we know four miles farther along the road.

We had never taken in any stranger strays for the night, but we had him sit down and eat some supper and soon saw that we were going to ask him to sleep the night. "I'm clean," he said. "No bugs."

He was sixty-four years old, and he had walked at least twenty-five miles during the day—all the way from Job's Pond. He had been a lumberjack in the woods of Oregon and worked in the western wheat fields. He told us about his childhood in the southern mountains. "My mother wove my clothes on a hand loom. There was only mountain tracks to travel on, by horse and buggy or on horseback. The roads followed the creeks. Most generally the road was in the creek or the creek was in the road."

He slept on a couch in the living room, rolled up in a blanket. In the morning he had breakfast with us, though he couldn't conceal a feeling that we ate breakfast at an ungodly late hour. It was nice the way he left us, not thanking us overly much, not too grateful, just polite and sturdy and pleasantly matter of fact. This was the way things are meant to be, his broad back seemed to say as he swung off along the road north, his gait strong and assured again.

55

10

THAT NOVEMBER was gray and lowery and dismal. Dark clouds
scudded over the chimney-top day after day, with sleet and icy
winds. The torn lake was too harassed and churned to freeze,
though the air was cold enough to freeze the gizzard of a goose.
Waves beat the rocks, and spray froze on the shoreline trees. At
night the stars glittered as hard and small as in the dead of winter.
We had but three partial days of sunshine the whole month.
Every now and then the dark sky would spit a little snow that
lodged in wheel tracks and heelprints and frozen plowed fields,
emphasizing their iron, winter barrenness. I used to look across
the black desolate hills and wonder how in Heaven's name they
could ever have been green and fertile, with sweet clover and
timothy waving in the wind. We probably have the worst Novem-
bers of any region in the world, unless perhaps it is the Aleutian
Islands. December when the snow comes, and February, the moon
of blizzards, are far more friendly, to my way of thinking.

You know that poem of Thomas Hood's:

> No sun—no moon!
> No morn—no noon—
> No dawn—no dusk—no proper time of day—
> No sky—no earthly view—
> No distance looking blue—
> No road—no street—no "t'other side the Way."

No warmth, no cheerfulness, no healthful ease,
No comfortable feel in any member—
No shade, no shine, no butterflies, no bees,
    No fruits, no flowers, no leaves, no birds,
        November!

That's the way November is in Horseshoe, but this year it was worse, because we were waiting for a baby, our second, and he or she was three weeks late. We had a dear friend staying with us and she was a wizard at taking care of the house and seeing to Kim. Kay was strong and well and doing most everything herself anyhow. We shouldn't have complained, but it was a long month just the same, with the usual winter cosiness gone because of the uncertainty about the babe.

Kay was kind of exasperated about the baby's lateness. She had been an obstetrical nurse for a long time and knew all about babies and mothers who got their dates mixed. She wanted to be as little trouble as possible.

We had made all arrangements to go to the little hospital at Greensboro, twelve miles away, where a fine young doctor named Holmes was working up quite a big practice. Kay had seen a lot of his work and was convinced that he was an unusually good man and as competent as all get out, in spite of being only twenty-eight. He had set up in the country on purpose because of the great need for good doctors in the rural regions. He knew it was tough sledding in a money way, but he was fighting it out nevertheless. It was he who had founded the little hospital at Greensboro by forming an assocation, putting in his own cash, and getting a lot of other people to contribute.

Late one gray afternoon toward the end of that gray November Kay came rolling in to the room where I was working at my desk and put her hand on my arm. "Let's go to Greensboro, shall we?" she said.

So, here it was. The touch of her hand made me shake.

"Is the prospective father doing as well as could be expected?" she asked solemnly.

"Yes," I said, wishing we had a phone so I could notify Greensboro to get things ready, wondering whether the Buick would start in the cold. We had decided that babies are nothing. Kay had said, "It's as natural as getting tired and sleeping. People make entirely too much fuss." That sounds good, but it doesn't cut much ice when the time comes.

"There is no hurry," she said. "I'm only having little pains."

I threw on my coat anyhow and ran out to try the car. I had a way of leaving it balanced on a knoll in front of the barn so that just a small push would send it rolling into the road and down a fair-sized hill. I had the gear lever in high by this time, of course, and midway down the hill let out the clutch and off she went with a bang. "God bless you," I said to my fine old junk heap. While I had the car running, I drove to the mill Village and telephoned Greensboro. Miss Vorst, the nurse, sounded just as crisp and jaunty as though I had asked her to go to dinner and the theater or something. "Yes, we'll have everything ready. Isn't that fine? All righty, bye-bye."

Things were coming along when I got back to the farm, and we couldn't leave any too soon to suit me. Kay bundled up and got into the front seat without any trouble. The chains were clinking (we usually wore out two sets a winter) and the cracked side curtains were flapping. It was just about like any other day, till this woman beside me hunched up and uttered a small sigh and then said, "That's better. Now, you don't have to race. This will probably take a long time and you must take it easy because this is just a natural phenomenon like eating your breakfast."

"Yes, sure," I said.

"I remember the taxi drivers when I was in the obstetrical ward at Sidney Hospital," she said. "They'd come tearing in hollering for stretchers, rolling their eyes, shaking all over. We'd race out to the taxi and there was mama, calm as mud, chewing gum, saying, 'The pains have stopped. I guess it was only false labor. Probably he better take me home again.'"

I really didn't know what to say to this, and felt quite tongue-tied.

She hunched up now and then or stretched out. Once she asked me to stop. "There, that's better, it's gone away again," she said, and we drove on.

All the mudholes were frozen hard, fortunately for us. After three or four centuries we drew up at the door of the little white hospital of this populous summer town, now so empty.

The five-bed hospital smelled of ether already. "Hello," said Miss Vorst. "Glad to see you. Business has been mighty dull around here. Dr. Holmes will be over pretty soon. Would you like the big front room, Mrs. M.? Come on up. Do you think you can make it?"

She led the way upstairs and Kay made it, with a pause halfway.

It is so eternally absurd to be a father waiting in a waiting room. Everything possible has been said about it. Why, and a lot of whys. The doctor came. Darkness came. For the first time in four years Daisy was going to miss getting milked, by the look of things. The night crawled like a black slug. Hours passed, but they didn't seem gone. I sat in the waiting room reading a copy of *Hygeia* magazine. The sentences looked peculiar, and even the paper felt queer. Dr. Holmes, an earnest, sandy-haired young fellow, made an examination every eon or so. "Things are fine," he said. "Just fine. You comfortable here? Don't you want to have a nap on the couch there?"

"Thanks, don't worry about me," I said. Dr. Holmes disappeared into some inner lair at the back of the hospital and there kept quiet.

Kay had told me that he was a very fine obstetrician, and she could spot one when she saw one. In her nursing days in various frontier communities she had delivered more than thirty babies, with no doctor to help, and she was what you might call an expert.

59

I had believed her when she said Holmes was good, but right now it seemed to me he looked hideously young. I know that he was a well-meaning man, because I had often had long talks with him about cooperatives and country medicine. We had exchanged all kinds of books, and I had been driving with him on the rounds of his cases and listened to his tales of the countryside. That was all very well, but why had we delivered ourselves into the hands of this half-fledged youngster?

I went upstairs again to kneel by the bed and say hello, casual, merciless, while her hair darkened with sweat as the pains laid hold of her. And she between pains explaining how it was, timing them. She glanced at her wrist watch at the onset. Then her hands clenched and her eyes closed, and she was gone away. She looked at her watch, relaxing all over. "Ten seconds they last now. That's good. I was afraid they'd go away." she smiled. "Funny, it seems like five minutes. Dr. Holmes says he hardly ever has seen anybody who could time her own pains—that is accurately. Nobody could, except with a watch. He was telling me—here's another, hold fast."

She glanced at her watch, turned her face away, every muscle grew rigid, and she was gone again into the pit.

It went away. She rested again, glancing at her watch as her muscles loosened. "A good one that time. The bad ones are the good ones. They do the business. Dr. Holmes was saying how funny it is about timing pains. He gets a call. 'Come right away.' He asks how long she's been in labor. 'Three, four hours,' they say. He goes, he sees the woman—wait a minute."

She turned her face away again and knotted up, no different from a crippled she-wolf. While the pain was lessening she looked at her watch.

"He asks the woman how frequently her pains come. She says about every half minute. He asks her how long they last. 'About five minutes.' So he gets out his watch. Her pains are coming once every four minutes, not every half. And they last six seconds, instead of five minutes. This happens to him over and over again until he has come to expect it. I've seen it too. It's perfectly understandable. The woman thinks it's all over, and she has hardly begun. Here comes another one."

It crawled over her and stayed and stayed, and lessened and went away. I had not known her hands were so strong as that.

Nurse came in brightly to see, "How are we getting on? First rate?"

Kay said, "Knot me up a sheet to yank on, nurse, please," quite matter of factly.

Nurse busied herself tying a sheet to the foot of the bed. She made talk brightly whether the pains were on or not. Then she went away. The sheet began to tighten as though it would rip with the strain.

"Where is the doctor?" I said.

"He's asleep, poor man. He was out all last night on another baby case."

Oh, so he was asleep, eh?

The sheet commenced to tighten again. She pressed her lips together tight and did not make any sound.

"If you breathe through your mouth it lessens the pain a little, it relieves the pressure somehow," she said. "But it's no good. It only prolongs things. There was a funny Irish nurse in a hospital I was in once, and she used to say to screeching mammas, 'Close yer mouth, Mother. Nobody ever had a baby with 'er mouth open,' very fierce. It's true too. Here's another. Go away now, please—"

I waited, looking at the ceiling, which was quite white and smooth.

"Go away now. I don't like you to see me this way too much. I'm all right. You don't understand this business. Come back after awhile."

I was away an hour, pounding the frozen road. The stars glittered in the icy sky. I began to run till the sweat ran down my

61

back, and it was good to run, not to get anywhere, but just to be running. Are you tired of walking, brother? Then run awhile. Are you tired of living? Then die and see how you like it. I decided that probably it would be a boy who would get rich and choke on his dollars, or a poet who would starve on his poems and beg for a job he detested and be chained to it by the exigencies of love till there was no love in him. Then he'd be turned loose when it was too late and told to play in a world where work drives people mad and leisure drives them madder still. Or maybe it would be a girl. If she was beautiful, her beauty would be her undoing; if she was ugly that would finish her. Some world! I picked up a branch by the roadside and hammered it against a tree till it broke. The stars were very small and cruel, and they glittered like teeth.

Back in the warm waiting room I listened. She was still alive.

Dr. Holmes stood on the stairs all in white, white gauze mask too. "How do you feel?" he said. "Would you care to help us? Things are coming along now. It might be good if you'd manage the ether mask for us. Do you feel equal to it? Are you affected by the sight of blood?"

It was war then! "Sure, glad to help," I said, and felt steady as a rock. While they were dressing me up and putting a mask on me, Holmes said, "I don't know whether she told you. It's a breech delivery. Nothing very unusual, but I'd be glad to have nurse handy in case I want her. I'll show you how to drop on the ether, and that will leave nurse free."

Nurse put a drop of castor oil in each of Kay's eyes. "It protects against the ether," she said.

"The mask goes this way," Dr. Holmes said. "Drop some on now. I'll tell you when to stop."

"I can tell him," said Kay. "Begin. Some more, MORE. . . . Nuf."

"Again, oh, oh."

"Again . . . nuf.

"You're doin' fine. Again, more. . . ."

"Watch my finger. Don't give me too much. More, MORE, MORE!"

This went on for a long time and I watched her finger and dropped on the ether when she raised it, then stopped when her finger fell. She seemed to have better command of her finger than of her voice.

"The hot cloths, Miss Vorst," Doctor was saying. "Everything is fine."

"Everything is fine," I said, though she couldn't seem to hear me. She twisted her face away, but I pressed the mask on firmly and let the drops fall fast. When her finger fell I stopped.

She screamed again and again.

"Give her more," said the doctor, and to her he called, "Breathe in and out, open your mouth, breathe deep, cry as loud as you can. Fine, fine." He said to me, "Give her more. Put 'er right under, right under."

The drops kept falling and she sighed and drifted away.

It was a boy and he was alive.

I didn't feel like celebrating and passing around cigars. There was nobody to celebrate with and I was glad of it. In the country you have to be self sufficient sometimes.

She slept all that day and most of the next day too. A week passed and it was evening and visiting time. Every night when I came to see her she lay in the bed looking more radiant and still stronger. "Bliss," she said. "Pure, unadulterated bliss and mountains of milk. You can't know how wonderful it is."

"You sure look fine."

"The reward is not so great for you," she said. "I lie here and I'm so happy I can hardly stand it. Isn't the baby a bouncer? You don't think much of him, do you?"

As a matter of fact I was a little worried about the baby, for even though it was our second one and I was supposed to be

63

pretty much up on these matters, he looked kind of inhuman to me. "He's a grand little fellow," I said. "He's got all his arms and legs and everything."

"You hypocrite. Fathers never like their kids much till they're about six months old," she said, smiling blissfully. "You'll see, that's how it'll be with you. I'm so happy now. Santa Claus will get around to you too, but he'll be about six months late, so don't be discouraged."

She laughed she was so glad. "You can't understand this and no man ever will be able to. Accept as I do, and believe me when I say it's worth it. The only way you can understand me and this business is to realize that you can't possibly ever understand. Understand?"

She held out her arms, and her fierce maternal beauty and strength went through me like a twenty-volt current.

"You know a lot, don't you," I said."

"Yes, indeed."

I had supposed she'd have a weak back or a cracked pelvis or something awful at this point. But it wasn't so.

When I left for home the world seemed kind of different. The stars were glittering in the sky as on that other night. They seemed milder, though, and the Milky Way was a scarf of jewels across seas of jewels. I drove along over the creaking snow that sounded like miles of canvas ripping, and I decided in a couple of hundred years I'd probably begin to catch onto things if I lived that long.

11

TODAY as I was walking home down the long hill north of our house, I heard Zack Tyler a long way off plowing his stony, stone-walled field. I stood by the fence and watched him, but not very long, because it doesn't seem right that one man should loaf while another works so hard. He saw me and nodded, but did not stop. What do writer chaps know of the inertia of the unturned ground. Will words turn it?

The reins were round his neck and there was sweat in the seams of his face though the wind was cold. Every minute he must turn out for a rock. "Gee, Tom, gee! Come up you, Jerry!" or stop the team and shout, "Whoa you!" and lift the plow. It doesn't take very sharp ears to hear him plowing a quarter of a mile away. Occasionally the plow-point catches on a buried ledge. These are the bad ones. But he has a rough chart of them and their depths in his mind. He's taken his soundings and his bearings and he knows this field as a pilot knows the channel to a harbor. He sails his sharp-prowed silver boat around his loamy sea and hardly ever bangs her on a sunken reef.

Words again, you see.

"Got your spring's work done?" he hollered.

"No," I said, and scurried like a rabbit.

The very first autumn I spent three weeks cutting firewood with him on his sugar place. Most of the trees we felled were yellow

65

birches that were shading out the maples. He was not so young as he had been, and he needed somebody to help him, especially on the other end of the crosscut saw. He had horses and a wagon and sledges and wedges and skidding chains and such, so that about all I had to bring was an axe. We cut enough for the two of us, there among the ferns and maples. The mornings were frosty and the noons were warm. They were happy days, pulling the crosscut saw with old Zack, smelling the sharp birch shavings, seeing the woodpile grow. We'd be trying to split a four-foot stick of curly birch with the wedges, a mean one, and get three wedges stuck in it. "Tougher 'n bull beef cent a pound," he'd say. The log was a big one, too heavy to lift onto the table of a buzz saw. So we'd knock the wedges out of it and saw it into chunks by hand. "There!" he'd say. "We'll dump those chunks into the heater stove *without* splittin' 'em. Stove'll straighten 'em out."

Our two sons had whooping cough that winter, and Zack was always dropping in to give advice on the subject. "You want to rub some skunk oil on his chest," he said. "Don't suppose you got any skunk oil. Wave some burning chicken feathers in the room, and wrap his stummick in newspaper bands soaked with kerosene." He had brought up three or four children himself and knew all about it. Next time he came to see us, he brought a small bottle of skunk oil. Neighborly, he was.

He had an ex-wife, now separated, of whom he lived in mortal terror. His first wife, Daisy, had been his true love. After she died, he grew very lonely, and in a moment of indiscretion he had taken unto himself a termagent named Ceelie. Ceelie seemed always to be living in some different township round about, and Ceelie had a flair for picking up new men, briefly. Ceelie claimed that some of the furniture in Zack's house belonged to her. He claimed it didn't. Every time he left his house, even to go out into the fields close by, he locked all the doors and windows, he was so afraid Ceelie would come with a truck and empty his house, as she had threatened to do. He said that before she went away for keeps,

66

she had burned down one of his outbuildings in a fit of rage. Every time he went out he expected his whole place to be a smouldering ruin when he returned.

Zack had a curious lack of perspective regarding national current events. Horror, sudden death, blood and gore were his newspaper fare. We'd hear the buggy wheels creak outside the house, and a loud "Whoa!" In came Zack, waving a paper. "Did you hear about the man got cut right in half, blood all over the street?"

"What's all this about," says Kay in what she thinks is a reassuring tone.

"A train run over 'im. Cut um right in half. Right straight acrost the stummick!"

"Oh come, where was all this?

Zack waves the paper vaguely. "Oh, I dunno. Chicago or one of them places."

Zack loves better than anything to ride in a car. He has never had one, can't drive one. But, providentially enough, who should come along to fill this need but ourselves, right next door. He is always asking us to drive him somewhere. And it's worth it for the sake of the local lore he recalls as we wind through the countryside. Often and often we have set out for Newport or Barton by the crookedest roads we can find, with Zack along doing the honors.

From the backdrop of the hills a whole generation of people step out and walk and work and talk for him. He has taught me, such as I am, to swing a scythe, encouraging me, telling me, "Why, when I was no bigger than a pinch of snuff we'd go out to mow the swale. My father'd come behind me, tellin' me, talking to me till I cried. You can't learn to mow by hand in one day, or two neither." It is he who has shown me that storm windows make good cold-frame covers, come April; that cardboard cartons will do for wallboard in a pinch; that a melted-up phonograph record will patch a small crack in a storage battery; that old jar rings will hold on broken overshoes; that drive shafts from auto junk yards

67

made the finest crowbars. As we go, he embroiders the countryside.

By the side of the road we pass a large graveyard. "Mmm," he says. "More people dead than alive in this town." Two trucks were there, a pair of horses yanking out thorn ash bushes by the roots, two men with scythes were clipping round the headstones, another with a lawnmower, another on his knees scissoring grass blades underneath the fence. "They're puttin' new life in that place," he says.

On the road across the mountain we pass four old farms that are in ruins, burned out, and there are many more on the other roads around, with fields growing up to bushes, fences all but gone. "They got burned out—now let me see, it was the year—" And we ride on, and a few miles beyond we come to another and another. He knows the histroy of each one, whose father built the place, what happened there. He remembers how the berries used to grow thick in their back pasture, and the times his mother and father went up there and camped, the time the sheriff attached a load of rock maple logs, the time the horses ran away. And then—"They got burned out. They moved away."

"Where'd they move to?"

Sometimes he knows, but generally he says, "I dunno."

I ask him why they didn't build it up again; their old home that they'd worked over and improved and loved and hated and made plans over for generations. Why didn't they use the insurance money to build it up?

"They couldn't. It costs $3,000 to build a good barn. It costs $3,000 to build a little house. There's six thousand. Well, they can go off and buy a better place for three thousand than they can build for six. It didn't used to be so.

"Now here's a place. Silas Groslet lives there, moved there ten years ago. He's only got ten cows. Hillside farm, ledges, soil not very deep. The government would call that a submarginal farm as sure as shootin'. But he gets along. He's got a good team. He and his wife get out around a little bit fer a visit. He ain't got any

68

mortgage, and he don't owe a nickel to nobody. There's plenty of valley farms five times as big as that, with richer land, that have failed up, the bank's got 'em long ago. Now what do you make of that? I ain't sayin' that there ain't plenty of poor farms so poor that nobody could make a livin' off 'em, but I'm tellin' you, Mister, there's such a thing as submarginal men too! What's the government gonna do with *them*. There's plenty of men that couldn't make a livin' off the best farm that was ever cleared.

"Here's a farm that Anson McIntyre used to own. His father was a horse trader, made a pile of money at it. Sold a pair of thoroughbred horses once to royalty in Europe, kings or somethin'. Anson was a trader too. He'd trade anything he owned. He had it in his blood. He had five wives 'fore he got through. When he come back from his honeymoon with No. 5, he climbed into the front seat of the stage that waited at the station. His wife got in behind. 'Well, Anse,' says Bill the stage driver, 'be ye satisfied this time?'

" 'Ain't made up my mind yet,' says Anse. 'But I tell ye. If I ain't, I'm going' to keep swappin' till I be.'

"You see them hills up yender? We used to raise a lot of wheat right here in Vermont when I was a boy. Along them ridges was solid wheat fields, and they've all gone back to woods again now. There's cellar holes up there so full of trees you couldn't find 'em. Everybody had his own flour milled them days. I remember when the first man around here bought some shipped-in cattle feed. Boughten feed! We thought the end of the world was come. Now everybody buys feed. Well, I was tellin' you, we raised wheat. And we made money at it. Then they started raisin' wheat out west. They shipped it east. They raised so hang much wheat they put us out of business.

"Well, so we started makin' butter. We sold cream and raised hogs on the skimmed milk. We set up butter-makin' creameries in all the towns around. And they made money, and the farmers made money. And I'll tell you another thing that was different from today. The money them little creameries made—it went back into the town. It helped pay the taxes, it made the storekeepers prosperous. People could buy things. Now most all those little independent creameries are busted, bought out by the companies in Boston. And all that profit we produce here—it goes off to the city and we never see it here anymore.

"Be that as it may. The westerners and middle westerners saw that we was makin' money here makin' butter. So they took to makin' butter. They shipped it east from farther than Wisconsin even. And like always, they made so hang much butter they cut their own throats as well as ours. Only, they could stick it out longer than we could, because they had bigger farms and better land. So we gave up makin' butter and we started shipping' raw whole milk, mostly to Boston. And that paid us very good for awhile.

"But soon the west and middle west got onto it. And, like always, they flooded the market. They shipped it east in tank cars. I tell you, Mister, the west has ruined Vermont. And now look at this new farm plan. Soil conservation my eye! New England voted against it solid. We get nothin' out of it. But they with their one-crop system and their mismanagement and their greed— they've got their land about half ruined. So now the government's goin' to reward 'em for it, and we got to help foot the bill."

I tried to tell Zack about China and its millions of acres eroded beyond repair, about 60-foot gulleys that are growing in Georgia and South Carolina and northern Mississippi, about the dust bowl, about the ruined civilizations that have sunk in sterile dust. But all those things are a long way off.

12

SOMETIMES IN WINTER there comes a spell of snowstorms and sunshine and terrific contentment. On snowy afternoons there is a special blessedness in saying, oh it is too snowy to chop wood this afternoon. And the gray snow sifts down, and one takes off one's boots and sits by the fire and is glad of the way wool socks smell; and a pie is baking in the oven, and the gray snow is sifting down.

Or one gets tired of that and goes out into the silent woods where the snow is whispering down through the bare branches, and plugs through the drifts, up the hills, past the cliffy ledge that is almost always clear of snow, in among the thick firs, across the brooks that are filled so deep you wouldn't know they were there. Here is the place where I had a fire yesterday. One stands on the cold hill in the icy wind looking off across the dimness at the shadowy mountains lost in the snowstorm, and one thinks. What does one think of? Oh, nothing much, just thoughts. And then it's good, going home to the fire and the creeping night, and Kim home from school on his skis, his cheeks very red, and he very hungry, and the darkness comes, and one is glad everybody is home over the twelve-foot drifts. It is simple and it is enough.

It's a contented existence, to write in the mornings, and ski in the sunny afternoons. Skis, like canoes, are molded, made beautiful and slender by the necessities of use, I often think as I snap them on and slip down the lovely, lonely hills where there are no tracks. Often in the park-like expanses of the maple sugar woods I scare up a rabbit and watch him go hopping away to hide under a brush pile somewhere. When a get tired, I sit down by a tree, make a fire maybe, and look across the blue, blue distances, across the sad old rocky hill farms and see the Green Mountains sticking up against the sky. Then home at evening under one of those flaming, powerful, heart-rending sunsets, to a big supper, warmth by the wood stove. Outside, the trees are cracking with the frost, and inside, there are furry clusters of frost on the nailheads by the door. That makes a hot buttered rum slip down all the smoother. We pull up our chairs and read after supper, and most any book seems good. If it is a truly fine one, it touches us and influences our lives. If it has gaps, we fill them in and don't care. If it is a skimpy, poorly put-together one, I enjoy it all to pieces because it makes me feel such confidence that I can write a better one than that. Then sleep, sleep so deep and log-like that it is one blessed utter blank. And in the morning there is new snow, no tracks, a clean slate again.

And if it seems good to us, then it seems good to us.

One of the great advantages of being a writer is that nobody can down you for long. Your proof of your pudding is always demonstrable. Your trade is demonstrating it, and the only capital you need is five cents worth of paper and ink. To prove whether you can write or not, all you have to do is write something good, and it is seldom that anyone or anything can keep you long from writing. If you can do it, you do it, and if you can't, you just keep trying. So what is the use of worrying; it will take care of itself.

One of my greatest aids is the wastebasket. It always inspires me with confidence to think, "Well, I can throw it in the basket and nobody will see it, so why not begin?" If it is one of those bad days, I begin to scribble, and in a really desperate time I just begin by scribbling nonsense about the weather or any old thing. My favorite opening sentences are "What'll I write. I'm sure I don't know. What'll I write. I'm sure I don't know." Then something begins to come after awhile, something worthless, of course, if it is a bad day. But it is better to write six pages that are no good and throw them away than to write nothing. It makes tomorrow seem less formidable. There are good days too, when twenty-five pages will flow out practically without need of change. Writing is like quarrying rock, I sometimes think. But, as in the case of a real quarry, you have to have something to quarry it out of.

Most every other unsuccessful person except an unsuccessful writer can claim that it was because he didn't get a chance. Somebody wouldn't let him use their infra-red telescope and electric calculator; or somebody wouldn't let him try out new ways of refining alcohol from sawdust or reorganizing the sales technique of a corporation. Even small inventors have a fierce time to get hold of a turret lathe.

But a write either writes stuff that people will read or he doesn't. And no amount of wishful thinking what he might have done or would like to do has anything to do with it. This is even more true than it used to be—now that every third person you meet is a potential writer. Some become actual and most remain potential. Q.E.D.

Somehow I find all this very stimulating, in that you are engaged in a nice private war which you can wage till you die, if your guts hold out; and you don't have to wage it by means of an army of other guys.

I get my best ideas for writing when I'm farming, and my best farm ideas when writing. Milking cows is very fine for ironing out plot difficulties. There is something soothing and stimulating to the mental processes in that rhythmic tug and squeeze, the quiet physical rote movement of it, the cow's warm flank, the smell of hay, the white streams building up in the pail. Every influence is physical, including the munching of Daisy's jaws and the flick of her tail. I think of the early days of my inexperienced milking when most of the milk went up my sleeves, of the days when it

73

took one solid hour to fill a pail. Balanced there on one leg of the milking stool, I have no need to think of anything at all. It is a time of complete calm. Am I not already doing a useful job, squeezing out this warm and foamy essence of nourishment for my children? A sense of being a peasant—clod-like and one with the earth—comes to me. I do not think, I am not required to think, there is no necessity to think. All conscious effort, all self-consciousness, and all the natural blocks are gone. Consequently I sit there teeming with story stuff. It flows through me as though I were a stranger and bystander, amused, non-recording, not concerned. I can't wait to get to a desk where I can set it all down. But after a little while at the desk I get thinking about cows again, and how will I get another, and how can I raise the money to seed some more field in order to keep her in the manner to which she is accustomed.

I figure that the human is a contrary animal and the only way to take advantage of his peculiarities is to work in rather peculiar ways. You have to sidle up to a desk in a strategic way or the thing won't serve you. It is no use to advance on a desk frontally and plump your elbows on it and say, "Now I will write something. I will think of something. It will be good." All is lost that way. You can sit for a week. The best way to write is hoeing corn or chopping wood or milking cows or walking the roads. The boots I've worn out writing books! I can well understand the New York author who walks his books. For him Fifth Avenue and 72nd Street is not Fifth Avenue and 72nd Street but will be forever the place where he decided to kill off Uncle Wismer or let Isabella have a baby. The countryside hereabouts is dotted with such invisible monuments. You have to be very peculiar to make the human peculiarities work for you, and that is why authors are usually considered a little bit queer. Really, they are the only sane ones, of course.

Hoeing corn on a hot day is one of the finest incentives to writing. The dust is very dry and the hoe handle chafes and the shoulder blades drip sweat. A general sense of the desirability of inertia pervades the scene. I think of my cool, shaded room and my nice dark smooth desk and that beautiful white paper. How pleasant it would be to sit there in a chair with the pen traveling over the paper as blithely as a squirrel running from tree limb to tree limb. Soon I am there, filling up the pages most happily hour after hour, and the happiest part of it is a secret joy, shared only by me, that I can throw all this in the basket and nobody will see it because I don't care about *them*. After several hours of this idiotic game, it is a pleasure to go back to the cornfield and just sweat, no thinking. Ah, the bite of the hoe blade into the earth! and the green simple corn leaves which toil not, neither do they spin, and the fine simplicity of the hoe handle and the automatic bodily movement after long hours cramped in a chair! So I bounce blissfully from one to the other, wanting whatever I do not have, doing whatever I am not doing, and profiting and being happy thereby.

All this makes my farming a bit strange to the passerby, no doubt. He cannot know that I am fixing fence in order to iron out Chapter 17. All he sees is the holes in the fence. Somebody asked me once how I could afford to spend so much time mowing by hand, and I mumbled something about keeping the bushes down and keeping the fields fields. But really I like to mow with a scythe, and I'm glad this little place, with its swales and many odd corners of crazy little fields where a horse mower can't reach, needs lots of hand mowing. There's something dynamic and true about the shape and feel of a scythe. To hear and feel that steel blade sweeping through the dewy grass is a song on a summer morning. The grass lies down like a girl's skirts when she curtsies. And scything is very hard work. A couple of hours of it is good for three hours at the desk most any day.

Farmers tell me I can't make this rocky little place pay, but they don't know the half of it. Is there anything more inefficient, I often wonder, than the intensified mathematical efficiency that destroys people.

75

I always think that if I had a little capital to play with, I'd make a fortune buying and selling abandoned farms around here. They can be picked up very cheap. At first glance they look like a pretty discouraging proposition, as far as the house goes. But you look in the cellar at the great wall-rocks that the ox teams drew in, at the well all mossy, at the fine sound sills of first-growth spruce sound as a dollar, and you feel enthusiasm for restoration rising in you like a head of steam. So much limitless work has already gone into this place that—why it's nothing the little that would be needed to bring it back and save it. The eroding gullies, how they cry to be fixed. I would fix up places and give them away if I could. It's the intrinsic job, not a desire for property, proputty. How simple it is to patch a hole in a roof and save a house. You see where the roof gapes at the break of the eaves, and the plaster has fallen beneath. How the bushes are growing around the house. What a cinch it would be to fix it all instead of letting it go to ruin. A few days work now—instead of ruin for all eternity. You sit in the broken kitchen and imagine the kitchen junkets, how they picked up the kitchen range and carried it out onto the porch, how the fiddler sounded as he sawed out the reels, and the flare of a girl's dress as a French-Canadian boy swung her round.

Craftily I shall take advantage of the desire of the hand for the hammer in that millennial day when I have CAPITAL to play with. I'll fix the hole in the roof and patch up the plaster. I'll give the house one coat of paint, so that you see right away it needs another. But carefully I'll leave one corner of the porch sagging, and a board off here and there. The sagging line of porch that cries for straightening has an appeal that some men can't resist. I can see myself saying, "Of course you could fix up that porch in an hour or so. It would make all the difference." And the prospect will shiver once, helplessly, and buy the place just because he can feel the pinch bar and hammer in his hand and wants so much to straighten up that porch. Come to think of it, I'll sell places by knocking out the posts from under porches. The reason I really bought this place of my own was that there were so many things to fix about it, things that I could fix myself. Maybe it won't be so very blameworthy—my hooking a client or two whose hands ache for tools. Maybe the desire of the hand for the hammer and plane and saw should be assisted.

13

THAT WINTER I spent cutting wood in the deep snow down in our swamp. The snow is so deep in February in the swamp that you often sink into the white fluff to the waist. Branches are laden and spill onto your head. Snow gets into your mittens and down your neck. Logs, wedges, sledge, axe, saw, easily get lost in the stuff, and the work goes much slower than it does on bare ground. But I had an old pair of snowshoes that I didn't mind beating up, and there's something about the snowy swamp in February that makes it seem very wild and far away and pleasant. Though it was another world, as still as dream, I could hear sounds miles away— a team on the creaking road, a pump engine somewhere toward the Mill Village, another axe far off.

I wanted to make sure this spring that we had a whole year's supply of wood ahead. Early in the spring we would get a circular saw and crew gathered together and saw our whole big supply (perhaps twelve four-foot cords). Then I'd split it and let it dry and put it in the shed where it could dry some more till fall. It's like a great store of treasure, when you see it piled there, butt-on, all dry and ripe for the burning. It's only when you've lived through some of these winters that you can understand. I like cutting wood, seeing the chips fly, smelling the sharp tang of birch, balsam and brown ash. I like sweating in the icy winter air and making a mild contest with myself to see how much cordwood

I can cut and stack before dusk. It's quite an achievement to sweat in Vermont in February.

Another reason for finishing up fast was that horses to draw out the wood can't get into our swamp after the hard freezes are over. The swamp is underlain with big springs and oozy muck that bogs a team, and the only easy time for sleds and teams in there is early spring. To harden my roads, I had a fine system of waiting for a thaw. Then I'd tramp my roads, double track, sleigh width, very hard with snowshoes in the wet snow. Come the big freeze in a day or so, and that was the time. That frozen track was like a boulevard and would hold up a two-ton team of horses as firm as concrete.

It's surprising how many hundreds of thousands of cords of green wood are burned in the U.S. every year. I ought to know how inefficient it is, because I've burned plenty myself. You burn half again as much wood, probably. You warp your stoves, rust out your stovepipes and soot up your chimney with an iron-hard form of creosote that is very hard to get out. Thus the danger of chimney fires is much increased. It's a scientific fact that every time you put on a green chunk the moisture coming out of the wet stick exerts a tremendous cooling effect, and the heat and energy of your present fire is mostly used to cook the new fuel, whose energy goes to dry the next batch, and so on. You have to split the wood much finer, which means that it disappears much sooner. Every time you try to stoke up the stove, you cool it down, and what this does to your disposition is more important than all the rest.

All this lent drive to my axe—which had a whippy handle that I had shaved down myself. All this made the yellow shavings from the saw-cut seem like something new and wonderful. With reluctance I saw the sky darken and the purple tree-shadows lengthen and deepen in the increasing cold. Evening came, and I was pleasantly tired. I piled my logs so they would not get lost if another snow came on. My wet mittens were starting to get stiff as the sun went down. When I looked up above the treetops, the sky had grown coppery bright with a sunset that would close down in sudden dark. It was time to follow the path out of the swamp, up through the firs and along to the road. That plowed road always makes me think of Robert Frost's most New England lines of all his New England lines:

> A plow, they say, to plow the snow.
> They cannot mean to plant it, though—
> Unless in bitterness to mock
> At having cultivated rock.*

I followed the plowed road along toward home, a white trench with all the crests of its high-banked edges filigreed and lace-like with fragments of chunks that the plow-wing had put there (the mailbox was buried again, I noted). The lake and the fields seemed very white and open and cold in the dusk, after the green enclosure of the woods. The night wind was blowing already, here in the open, making the snow dust stir. Across the lake I could hear dairy farmer Sibley hollering at his cows.

Sometimes it hits me, the panorama of lake and hills, the crystal loneliness of it, the night cold coming down. And I stand there, to the knees in snow, feet half frozen, the crosscut saw eating into my shoulder. It's a spell like a trance, and still it won't break. The supper smoke is coming blue out of the chimney, and the window in the kitchen shows yellow. The house looks so incredibly cozy and desirable in the midst of this fiercely beautiful and merciless landscape, it is enough to tear your soul out by the roots. Into my mind comes the realization that here I am, now, out of all time and all space, here in this place. And I say to myself, This is my house. My woman. A baby. Two babies.

Simple things like that.

*From *Collected Poems of Robert Frost.* Copyright, 1930, 1939, by Henry Holt and Company, Inc. Copyright, 1936, by Robert Frost.

It was too cold for standing there any longer. I crunched into the woodshed and took a broom from the doorstep to brush some of the snow off myself. The saw on its nail on the woodshed wall jangled with the dull clang-ring of a very cold night. It is wonderful that people can keep alive here, I often think. And yet, of course, that is silly, because people keep alive all across Sweden and Finland and Minnesota and Maine and Dakota, where the winters are as cold as this or colder.

The warm kitchen and the handsome black stove seemed like a palace. The house smelled of apples from having had so many barrels of them stored in the cellar. But added to this was a touch of turnips and woodsmoke and blankets and crisped brown beef, and the biscuits Kay was pulling out of the oven. She had on a gingham dress that she should have thrown away years before, but we both liked it so much she kept sewing it up.

"Where's everybody?" I said.

"Kim's at the Phillips and baby has dropped off to sleep. I must wake him up too."

"Nobody to chaperone us?" I said. The warmth after the intense cold makes you feel half drunk for a few minutes. I took a chair by the stove and pulled her onto my knee. She had two pink spots on her cheeks from the heat of the stove.

"Your face is nice and cold and you smell of balsam," she said.

"I wanted to ask you something."

"You did, eh?"

"Yes I did."

"What makes you so serious?"

"I was standing outside and thinking about the work and the house and the woman in here, and things."

"Why didn't you come in, you dope?"

"I wanted to ask if you are happy here."

She threw the padded pot lifter onto the floor with a fine gesture of abandon, put her arms around my neck, and that was the answer.

81

14

A PLUME OF SMOKE goes up over the little Vermont town on the hill, and in sunny hayfields for miles around where the dew has just dried enough for raking, men look up and see it. They smile. "Pete Young's east piece has got soaked so many times 'tain't wuth puttin' in the barn. He's burnin' it up."

"I bet he's sore, Pa," says a boy on a horse rake.

"I bet he is," says Pa. "Gee up there, Tom. Now whoa!"

The morning breeze is blowing strong from the north, bending the upland grass, shoving the white clouds over the hills.

But the smoke rolls thicker, denser, till it stands up above the town like an awful threat, "It's Simon's house." "No, it's the school." "'Tain't. I can see the school roof. It's over beyond."

"Run 'em, boy," says Pa. "The rud's smooth enough. Good! Hustle and call Ma. She may want to go. Back out the car while I unhitch."

The screen door bangs, and Ma comes out untying her apron. "Maria's just phoned. Roger Clayton's house is afire. Hardcastle fire engine is on the way." She installs herself in the back seat of the Chevrolet, ready before the rest of them as usual, though she has twice as much to do, she thinks.

From miles and miles around they come, thousands of jobs thrown up this summer morning, birds left to sing alone in the fields, scythes hung on fence posts or tree limbs, horses unhitched and left to graze beside the wagon, hand rakes stuck erect in the swale, handle down, teeth up. A six-year-old boy, turning the grindstone on a mountain farm, straightens his back and whoops, and wonders whether it's right to whoop because a house is burning. The butter stands unchurned, the kettle boils dry on the stove. On every road a cloud of dust is traveling fast. Buggy wheels rattle, horns toot, the village church bell is ringing. Miles away the thundering exhaust and siren of the Hardcastle fire rig roll through the sunny deserted fields where daisies nod in the cool north wind.

Nearly a thousand people ring the burning house while half a hundred work on it. Only the ell part is afire, but inside the ell are four barrels of oil which Roger had stored for his roadscraper trucks. One by one the barrels catch alight with a roar of flame that soars a hundred feet into the air. Little children hide their faces and whimper. The crowd moves back. And now, summoned by the ever mounting column of smoke, more people come from other townships, old graybeards that never come down out of the hills except for the September village fair, barefoot boys on bicycles, puffing, big-eyed, wishing, as they draw near, that they were on the roof with Frankie LaBaye, in danger, in the public gaze, hacking in the heat, chopping, trying to chop the ell roof loose from the house, held up himself by nothing, it seems, but a few shingles.

Maidens who never before looked twice at Frankie clasp their hands. "Oh, make him come down."

But he will not come down. The Hardcastle fire rig has arrived, the limp hoses suddenly fatten, and Frankie is soaked and nearly knocked from the roof by a blast of water. His clothes stick to him, showing every muscle of his thick-set body. He looks down at the girls and grins, one foot supported on a nail. "Cool me off again," he hollers, and the firemen oblige.

"Think they can save 'er," says a wooden-legged man to a square-shouldered grandpa of eighty in a torn straw hat.

"Dunno. Oil is bad. How'd she start?"

83

"Rags they say. Oily rags. Went off by spontarious combustification they say. Thet's what they allus say. How'd *they* know? Kin they show me the rags, hey?"

Two girls ride up on horseback to join the throng. One of them stretches her hand and her face high into the air to cry, "Hiya, Nancy!" The girl she is waving to has on a picture hat and all her war paint so early in the morning. "How you been all winter?"

"Huh, summer folks," grunts the old man.

Like a stream of ants men issue from the front door of the main house with furniture. The second-storey windows are open, and mattresses and blankets are flying out. The town clown appears in the front doorway with a chamber pot and gets a wild yell from the crowd. The firemen are mad because the crowd is in their way. All the ell is outlined in sheets of flame, upon which the hose stream makes no impression whatever. Four men stagger down the porch steps with a heavy safe, two more with a sofa.

Haggard men drenched with sweat, their voices hoarse, their shirts cinder-holed, race past two women talking of a picnic. Lucy Wilton, the ex-school teacher, has dough on her hands. "Wilton wouldn't give me time to wash or anything."

Old Mrs. Small has on her usual three aprons. The other school teacher, Ernest Seton's wife, who is going to have a baby, is there too with a voluminous cape clutched tightly about her.

The house is severed, Frankie has descended safely at the last moment, the ell roof is falling in. The water is holding out okay. Maybe they'll save the main house. Most every woman is talking about what she was doing when the news came: "I was just sweeping down the stairs." "I'd just put the dinner on, and I know it will be scorched to a crisp." "The cows were in my flowerbed and we were driving them across to the brook lot. Harry left them in the road."

Mr. Thrigg rushes by, wild-eyed, drenched too, his hair in his eyes, and Mrs. Thrigg, looking proudly at her man, says to her neighbor, "Harold was here among the very first, and but for him

84

I don't know quite what would of happened. Some folks around here are not good fire fighters."

"Yes, and I was just feeding the baby," replies her neighbor. "Oh, don't look at her. She spills so." Baby has on an expensive pink crepe de chine bonnet and coat, under which lurks a fine collection of spinach and gravy.

A gang of boys on their bicycles are getting up a race around the white-fenced village green. They pedal past a steep-spired Colonial church at the far end that looks more picturesque against the emerald hills than any picture has a right to do. Many of the boys who live no more than four miles apart haven't seen one another since school let out in June.

The fire is dying. The hose men switch their nozzle toward a garage roof where a little fire has begun to char the shingles. One of the big old elms beside the smudged white house is scorched so badly it will die.

T. Eaton Harwood is there in the foreground, in white flannels, a Panama hat, clipt moustache. He is the owner of two of the three trim summer residences adjacent to the fire, southward and to leeward too.

"Then two thousand dollars you put into the village well, Mr. Harwood," says a farmer, "they was wuth sompthin' today."

"Yes, Jerry. I figure all three houses would have gone this morning had the water failed."

"That water them drillers got's as hard as a granite boulder, but it puts out fires, even if it won't wash clothes."

"Yes, we find our water-softener at Sunnymede effective, however," says T. Eaton. His wife is across the road with her Leica, standing on a tombstone in the village graveyard, snapping the crowd, the fire, both.

Some women with paper bags of food are sitting in the shade, eating and gossiping with their backs to the fire, making the scene even more like a fair. The young summer boys and girls have agreed to meet tonight at the Three Rivers dance.

85

A little girl with pigtails flying prances through the crowd with the last and final news bulletin. "Mrs. Roger Clayton has hysterics. She's screaming. Mrs. Roger ——"

The local minister and the first deacon of the church take each a chair from the huge assortment of furniture at the road edge, and carry it back into the house.

"I done my share a' ready," says a boy with a harelip, who strained his shoulder to put the piano under a distant maple tree. The farmers' cars begin to roll away. A hay wagon hitched across the street rattles off. The crowd thins. They go back to the hayfields, the garden weeds, the butter, the dinner, the dance. The wind blows, and a thread of smoke eddies over the soaked fire.

Late at night in a farmhouse in the hills, a six-year-old boy patters through the patches of moonlight to his mother's bed. "Ma, I can't sleep. I keep seeing the flames. It was so hot. What if *our* house should burn?"

She puts out her arm and rocks him. "Go to sleep. Fire is good and fire is bad, like everything else. You were lucky to see it. What if we hadn't taken you? Think of that. Think of swimming in the lake. Now go to sleep."

15

WE EARLY FOUND it necessary to keep a hog as the simplest way of using the skim milk left over from butter making. By and by we raised two hogs each year and a veal calf, and sometimes a lamb or two. There is nothing quite like milk for making them grow.

At hog butchering time, along in early December, Lyman, Lane and Zack and I each bring our hog and get together for a day of it. Occasionally one of us is missing because he isn't on speaking terms that year.

Somewhere out in the barnyard in a pile of rocks the fire is roaring under an enormous iron kettle. The hog is stuck, and I look away, because of all things this is the worst. Of late years I shoot mine through the head with a .22 first.

All that I'm useful for in this gathering of skilled technicians is the heavy rough work that doesn't require any brains. I mostly carry wood and water, and heave on the block and tackle. Lane has a handy maple limb for hitching the overhead tackle to. Lyman generally uses a sheerlegs tripod affair. I fill the barrel beneath the hoist with buckets of hot water, and when the hog is good and dead, a man raises the gambrel tendons and we hook the creature's hind legs into a double team neckyoke and hoist him up for a sloshing. He may weigh three or four hundred pounds, so this is where I am useful on the rope. The water must be just hot enough but not too hot, otherwise the bristles will "set." Zack always puts a little wood ashes into it. Then we all begin scraping the bristles off with dull old scrapers that look like candlesticks. If the water temperature has been right, the bristles tumble off in mats, and after a little more sloshing Lane and Lyman finish shaving the last hairs away with knives whetted sharp as razors. We can't seem to buy good knives anywhere, but we have some excellent ones homemade from worn-out files or broken crosscut saws.

Either Lane or Lyman is very good at dressing the beast, locating the various livers and hearts, and finally splitting the backbone down the center with a saw. They do the job with neatness and dispatch that makes it seem very simple, unless you have ever tried it yourself. All this while the great white carcass dangles from the pulleys, with a man holding each foreleg. Many pans and dishes are required for the intestine fat, heart, liver, kidneys, and tongue. The snow is tracked up, red here and there, dogs excited, horses nervous. The fire flares and smokes black as a pillar when I throw on a piece of old automobile tire—saved by a miracle from Old Man Bushwell's ubiquitous and almost irresistible pleading. No matter how cold the wind is on our freezing hands, no matter how prosaic the chipped enamel dishpans, the whole performance always has a certain ceremonial touch. The hooks, tools, knives and ways of doing things are standardized by conventions stemming from many centuries. This pig represents millions of others, singled out for sacrifice because man has found it will grow more meat on less feed than any other of the earth's creatures. The "melt" or spleen is our inevitable augury, examined with great care. If it is long and thick, we will have a long hard winter; if short and thin, a brief mild term of cold; and so on. "Never saw it to fail," says Zack, and I, a modern who never saw it do anything else, keep quiet as befits the unskilled labor.

So it goes, with time out for dinner in the farmhouse, one of those extra-sized dinners, sometimes of fried liver.

Having done up three or four hogs, it is time to depart. Usually Zack and I go along together, our four unwieldy half-hogs laid carefully in the back of his wagon, and he, with one hand on the reins, describing all the way down the hill how the scent of fresh-killed pork practically always makes horses run away.

At home I carry the 150-pound halves in on my back and lay them on a table in a cold end room. Kay and I manage from this point on by ourselves. Uncle Hank bequeathed us a yard-long meat saw, to which we have added as our principal aid U. S. Department of Agriculture Farmers' Bulletin No. 1186, called "Pork on the Farm." It is one of the most useful pieces of literature imaginable. Full of pictures, diagrams, and the clearest of copy, even we found no difficulty in following it. First we pry out the leaf lard; then, when the carcass has cooled, I set to with the meat saw in one hand and the diagram entitled "Cuts of Pork" in the other and mark our pig off as though he were a log of wood. We had some odd-shaped hams the first year, but they were edible. The bacon, the shoulder butts, the spare ribs, the pork tenderloin, the hams and fatback—it's all as simple as ABC and much easier than a picture puzzle or learning to play poker. The book tells how to render out lard, how to make sausage and head cheese, how to pickle and smoke hams and bacon, and everything necessary. For days the larder groans with plenty, while we feast on tenderloin and chops, and the fragrance of cracklings fills the house.

We usually freeze some of the roasts, wrap them up, and bury them in the sawdust of the icehouse, where they keep for months. We found the government receipe for pickling hams and bacon a little too salt, so we altered it in subsequent years to suit our taste. My first smokehouse was a barrel with an old pan smouldering in the bottom, the meat suspended on strings, and a wet bag thrown over the top. We scoured the countryside for hickory bark to burn in our pan but later found that maple chips or corncobs do just as well. I almost burned up a barrel of hams and bacon when fat dripped into the pan and made the fire blaze up. After that I used a large packing case, with the smoke pot in one corner and no meat above it. By the third year we were curing the most delicious hams and bacon we had ever eaten—much better than those of our neighbors who had been doing it for generations. The neighbors were the first to comment on this, with a pleased air. They had taught us so many things, they were beginning to take pride in us, perhaps.

16

THE WINTER was long that year, and spring was slow in coming. Along about March I decided that splitting wood and wading through snow to the eyes were getting kind of hateful. Almost immediately it seemed essential to go to the city and confer with my publisher. After all, manuscripts and publishers were my business, weren't they? They certainly were, and I immediately discovered that a dozen urgent matters needed immediate attention in New York.

I put a few clean shirts in my bag, Kay pressed my good suit, and I set off through the snow, chilled to the bone already in my flimsy city clothes. I never checked my arctics till I reached Grand Central. Going up the long steps to the upper level, I saw an old gray-haired woman struggling with a heavy bag. Without thinking, I moved over to her, shifted my bag to the other hand and took hers, saying, "Your bag looks heavy. Let me help you."

The suspicion and outrage that gleamed from her eye made me remember a number of things I had forgotten. "Take your hand off that bag or I'll call a policeman," she rasped. Her fist knotted up on a half-raised umbrella and she bared her teeth like a lioness defending her cubs. A few listless individuals on the stairs came alive and pricked up their ears with the first faint signs of pleasure that had come to them in years. They drifted closer, with a view, perhaps, to protecting the embattled old harridan from my wanton assault.

"No offense, Madam," I said setting down the bag. "I only

wanted to help you." It was then I realized that I was truly in the city.

It is unbelievably strange, you know, to come from the country to the city after long months in the snow. You go about wide-eyed, looking into all the faces, individually, every one; you listen and hear and see and judge and weigh, noticing everything, accepting nothing. You stand in front of an electric-eye door and wonder if it is worth what it cost, and how it works—till the human stream pushes you on. Every noise, you wonder where it comes from and what makes it. The neon signs catch your eye irresistibly and you notice imperfections where someone forgot to paint the tubing black. Who was he and why did he forgot. To go to a morning movie with the night shift, the night firemen and watchmen, some steel workers in stiff helmets. To smell the five-and-ten-cent perfume again, and the steampipes and the mass smell of crowds—it's magically exhilarating, because you're there all alone, drinking it in. It gives you a kind of a lost-gone feeling too, no rocks, no trees, no snow, no one caring for you in the slightest, and you sit alone in the dark movie thinking thoughts that would never come to you in the country.

The novelty of it is overwhelming and depressing. It seems as though infinities of cold lost space ache all around you and all is lost, lost, as Thomas Wolfe and everyone and everything is lost that is not rooted in nature and growth and sunlight and wind. I remember a harassed parent who said to me once, "You know, don't you, that the only thing worse than having children is not having any children?" Here are the lost city millions who can never be freed because they don't want to be freed. And one wonders what to do and feels lost till he remembers that the world will roll on in unpredictable ways, following swings and swoops of action and reaction, and that as the city gets worse the country gets better.

All that is a trifle disconcerting as one goes about, examining the details of a lady's jewelry-and-natural-garden hat, a girl's one-eyed hairdo, the gum splotches on a subway car floor, a frozen fountain. Studying them all, accepting nothing, wondering, seeing them fresh, one is so sensitive, like a child, so uncalloused, that soon the million-ringed circus of interest brushes away depression, and one jumps with both feet into the maelstrom of things, things, OH THINGS.

My publisher takes me to lunch in a very subdued and elegant old joint where the lights are just dim enough, and the walls are all paneled with dark, polished wood that was ancient when Moses was a boy. And the waiter comes immediately and says to my publisher, "The usual?" and he says, "Yes," and it's all like the stuff that gets out of books into life and back into books again. And here I am on Mount Olympus for a change, instead of splitting wood.

My publisher is much concerned with Plot, and Suspense, and what he calls Artifice. He has to be or he couldn't stay in business long. They all have capitals, the way he says them. It is much more interesting when he gets talking about people. Mary Roberts Rinehart has a special pen she writes with, or used to, and she hides it so no one can make away with her magic. Wodehouse for years used as his indispensable instrument a broken-down typewriter and whenever it conked out, all was lost. There are some who can only write lying flat on their stomachs on special rugs in special houses. Others stand up to chiffoniers and refrigerator tops, poor devils.

"The universal cry from authors," says my publisher, "is always advertising. *Why don't you spend more money advertising my book?*" The reason is that there are some books that won't catch on, no matter how much advertising and promotion money they get. Others happen along that go like mad with practically no advertising. Sales are not in direct proportion to the amount of advertising and promotion. Says my publisher! "Advertising can stimulate demand for a book but it cannot create a large demand. Do you know that Dickens gave his publishers hell about the

Christmas Carol? He said his publishers had done such a skimpy job of advertising it that nobody would ever hear of it. It would die a-borning and be forgotten. Sad, wasn't it? Publishing is a risky gamble, and sometimes a publisher can't afford to take on more risks than he is already loaded up with. Oddities are the rule."

My publisher decided we ought to have another scotch and soda at this point. When it came, he said, "Did I ever tell you about Emil Ludwig?"

"No."

"Ludwig's biography, 'Napoleon,' was turned down by five New York publishers. It was something new in the way of biography and they couldn't see it. Finally Horace Liveright brought it out. It was a hit, the first of a number. Well, the money was rolling in, and the publisher thought it would be a friendly gesture to send along a few royalty checks, say once a week for a few thousand or so. And he did. Ludwig was down south somewhere, grinding away on another book. First thing you know, comes an urgent cry from Ludwig—For Heaven's sake stop those checks, they are ruining my work and poisoning my existence. Ludwig said he was accustomed to writing under financial pressure and that the weekly checks made it impossible for him to do anything. He made the publisher promise not to send him any royalty statement for at least a year. That's the way with authors. You never know what to do with them, and whatever you do is wrong. I myself have hit on the system of never writing an author anything less than a four-page letter. It makes him feel good. He goes around telling his friends that his publisher sends him four-page letters. Doesn't matter what you talk about—the weather, the World Series, children's schooling, anything so long as it's four pages."

One thing that enfuriates the publishers about authors is that the crackpots are always writing something different. They build him up, let us say, as a master of the sentimental love story. He

94

has a big success. Then immediately it goes to the big stupid's head. Do you think he will repeat? No. He gets the idea that he is a great tragedian, or a comic or god knows what. The public is standing around with its mouth open gasping for another sentimental love yarn with the names changed, when what should appear to our wondering eyes but a treatise on how to build rustic fireplaces, or a dirge in which everybody dies and nobody lives more than five pages. The publisher sighs and bravely faces his task. He tells the booksellers and the public that wonderful as the love yarns were, this man is remarkable, he can do everything. He can also build fireplaces and you'd be amazed how interesting Mr. Loveyarn's fireplaces are. To the great breadth and scope of his magnificent work he has added more breadth and scope and hosanna. Nobody pays any attention whatever to this. The booksellers buy the book and the book buyers buy the book convinced that here is some more dirt on how to extricate yourself from a hotel room when hubby returns and finds you in his wife's arms. Soon shrieks of rage begin to puncture the empyrean. It's a gyp, it's about how to build a fireplace. I want my money back. Bravely the publisher struggles on. No sooner does he get the irascible author established as a fireplace builder of consummate proportions, than the weathercock author is off studying the habits of tropical fish and trying to claim that they are interesting as all get out.

Never tell an author anything. That's the best policy. Never tell him his book is good, because if you do he'll keep the letter, and when the thing doesn't sell, as it may very well not—books being unpredictable even to publishers—he'll rush in to the office from the far reaches of Dakota or somewhere and say, Look, this convicts you from your own mouth. It is a fine book, and you have bungled it so that it will never be heard of.

On the other hand, never tell an author that his book is bad, unless you want to get rid of him permanently. For you never know when the poor creature will accidentally make your (the publisher's) fortune. Just tell him, "Dear Mr. Snodgrass: What a pleasure it has been to go through your new MS. We do feel that it is well up to your previous standard (noncommittal, you see) and a work of considerable promise. We are all pleased here to know that it is finished at last, and we feel keenly your weariness (God, if you only know how much you have told us about how empty you feel, how drained, how like a mother after three years' hard labour). We are all agreed that it is definitely promising, and though of course we depend upon you to realize that there is nothing more unpredictable than a book's success or failure from a financial viewpoint, you may be sure that we here will be behind it solidly (in some bar) and doing everything possible for it when publication date comes."

Eugene O'Neill is considered the model author because he almost never comes into a publisher's office. He writes his play, asks no advice about it, finishes it and mails it in without comment. That is the end of it. The publisher can do what he likes with it. That is really cricket as far as the publisher is concerned. Most authors, in a fever, walking the streets at night, cannot refrain from asking timidly at the end of three months whether the publisher thought it was good or not. But O'Neill is apparently of unusual fiber and toughness.

"Writers are queer it seems." I said.

My publisher is really a very nice guy. He smiled and nodded. "They have to be. The old metaphor of the mother to her child is still the best one. An author doesn't view his work with logic or with reason. It's something special, known only to himself. If you help him he is furious because you are trying to make him 'dependent.' If you let him alone, you are ignoring him, and he makes a special trip to town to demand 'at least the appearances of intelligent interest.' You know what would be nice?"

"What?"

"If publishers could dispense entirely with authors." My publisher smiled. "But unfortunately they can't."

My publisher is really a very nice guy.

Seeing people, eating food, walking here, riding there, it is all very exciting and pretty wearing. On a subway I see a gray-haired woman in thick glasses move over to a girl who has a baby. "Oh, you lucky, lucky, lucky," cooes the woman to the girl. The young girl mother beams and the baby kicks its feet. "What is it, boy or girl?"

"Girl."

"Oh you lucky, lucky, lucky. I haven't any. You lucky."

The lights flash, the taxis whiz, the trolleys clang and the subways scream. Slither, crunch, boom, whoop. And the interest is so terrific, the stimuli so powerful, that in a couple of days the farmer from the sticks begins to get very tired. He sees he musn't look into every face, he mustn't read every single sign, he mustn't weigh and question and share the joy and pain, or it will kill him. He must build a rind around himself and get callous, he must look with unseeing eyes and learn not to hear or smell or wonder, else it will kill him.

So then it's time to go back to the country again, very happy, very full of new ideas, very glad to see rocks and trees and hills and icy brooks again even from the train window. The whole countryside seems new, and its most blessed quality is that it bears looking at and listening to so well. You can look at it with wide-open eyes and find rest. Splitting wood was pure pleasure again when I got home.

17

I HADN'T BEEN HOME very long before I began to realize it was still March. The gray wild snow came swirling down, piling up in the wind, whistling dismally at a time of year when spring ought to be coming, at a time of year when roses are budding in the Carolinas, when everybody in Vermont has such a bellyful of winter that hardly anybody speaks to anybody else, when. . . . Well, at this critical juncture Mrs. M. announced one morning, "I'm going to Newport."

I knew she didn't mean Newport, Rhode Island—merely Newport, Vermont, a border town twenty-five miles above us, close to the Canadian line. It's the largest place that is close to us. Still I asked, "Newport? Why?"

"No reason. Just for my soul, that's all. I want to be somewhere else. So I'm going up there and stay two or three days in a hotel and look at the wall. Any objections?"

"None whatever," I said with great alacrity. "I think it is a very wise idea. Indeed I do." Mr. M. is not quite so dumb as he looks.

She had had a very long term of dishes and scrubbing and sweeping. The winter kept stretching out to the far edges of the infinite, and it didn't seem right that I should be the only one to go gallivanting. I urged her to go, by all means, and felt quite noble. I knew how it would be when she was gone, with dishes and dust and food and babies and pots and pans. I remembered a time when she had been sick and I washed twenty-six diapers in one morning. There is no doubt about it that women are wonderful creatures.

"I feel as though I must stay in a hotel," she said, "where I won't have to cook or make the beds or lift a finger. Isn't that silly?"

"Not at all. You go as soon as you want and stay as long as you like."

For several days the idea continued to ferment, and then she said, "I'm going. I can't help it."

The Buick was not running. She decided to go to Newport on the bus.

"But why don't you go to Boston or somewhere?"

"No, Newport's good enough, and when I get lonely I'll be able to get home quickly."

I saw her off, and sank immediately into a sea of detail. The meals were late, everything was dirty, the stoves needed stoking and the children ditto, all at once, all the time. Not to mention the cows and the hens and the pig. I had an idea that, once away, Kay would never come back, and if she did, she must be very blind and foolish indeed.

It was four days later when I saw her coming up the road and heard all about it. The first day hadn't been so bad. It was pleasant to be rolling up the Black River valley, doing nothing useful, seeing farmers' wives get on the bus, hearing them talk, feeling that one was different, though one was not.

The hotel room had bare walls. The town was empty and quiet with winter's repressiveness, nobody much on the streets, nobody much in the stores. The winking signs made you wonder how the shopkeepers ever made the money to pay for the electricity.

To the movies, but not much good. Everything seemed terribly quiet.

"Into the hotel lobby the first evening walked Mr. Osgood, the soul of hospitality—you know that friendly minister and his family—insisting I stay with them. I, alone in a hotel in their town! It was an insult to them. I told him no. Anyhow, what did I care

99

for their happy home life. I had come to stay in a hotel and that was where I was going to stay.

"In the morning I went shopping in those stores full of thousands of dollars worth of stuff but no people. I strung it out, but was finished by eleven. Went walking in the snowy hills outside the town high above Lake Memphremagog with a sandwich in my pocket. All day as long as I could. But it was only four o'clock when I got back. There was Mr. Osgood again in the lobby waiting for me. I thought it was wonderfully good of him to ask me again.

"So I went to the Osgoods' after all. Sons, daughters, dishes, meals, stoves, towels, family stuff—you can't get away from it. Mrs. Osgood knew just how I felt. They're the nicest people ever, and she's coming to stay with me someday."

Time passed pleasantly enough with the Osgoods, but there was no bus till four o'clock the next day. There weren't many passengers aboard when the elongated old Packard pulled out for south, and most of those soon got off. It was dark in the Black River valley, except for lights on the snow. Kay and the driver were the only two rolling down the valley. In wintertime the drivers often find the road long, and to shorten it they talk at great length with their passengers, discussing points of view, local Characters, cows, national politics or even the weather.

"You married?" he said.

"Yes."

This was followed by a long silence during which he seemed to be waiting.

"Where d' you live?" he continued finally.

"Horseshoe."

"How many cows?"

"Two."

"Two!"

"Yes, only two."

Another long wait. "Got children?"

"Yes."

"Hm-m." Another long wait.

At last the driver opined, "Say Mrs., you must be all set at home."

"Why do you think so?"

"This time a year every woman gets on the bus gives me an earful. Troubles. '*He* don't do this. *He* oughta done that. I sez to him I says 'f you ain't satisfied with me no better'n I be with you, I pity you.' Or else it's kids. Kids sick. Kids fight. Uncle's barn boots daubin' up the kitchen floor. What's the matter at your house, Mrs.?"

"Nothing."

He gave her a long look. "Is that true?"

"Yes."

He was not entirely convinced, though. "You sure don't say much. Don't happen very often."

At Pike's corner he let her off, in the eternal snow, in the glow of yellow headlights. The bus was empty and he'd be going on alone— make the whole run to Montpelier alone maybe.

"So long, Mrs."

"So long, driver."

It wasn't very far across the end of the pond, along the road in the snowy dark, only about a mile. And then she was there, and nobody knows who was gladdest.

18

WE HAD a big bowl of raspberries for supper tonight and gave away another bowlful to some neighbors. We have luscious ones this year, and like most things on the farm, they have a history. Everything has a history.

Our raspberries are all tied up with the blacksmith down the road. He's an outspoken individual who's had a good many economic ups and downs like the rest of us. He's always been crazy mad about horses, horses of his own, racing trotters. Sometimes when his family had hardly food and clothes enough to get along on, he'd be carefully graining and grooming two of the most beautiful trotters you ever saw. And they were the pride and joy of his whole family too. No one in the family would have cared to trade the horses for a grand piano and five barrels of flour or two boxes of rock candy or anything else. That's the way they were; they were a unit. Smithy had a two-horse buggy and a two-horse sleigh. He had trained his blooded horses to run as though the devil were after them whenever he pulled lightly on the reins. This gave a dramatic quality to his entry and exit from town, he standing up pretending to pull back on the reins with all his might, while the two beautifully matched horses thundered down the road as though they were running away and he couldn't stop them. The fact that all this was a vestige, that even here in this little Vermont town hardly anybody has driving horses any more, made the flying equipage of this man all the more exciting. About the only money he earned with his pair was driving a doctor from Hardcastle on his rounds when mud or snowdrifts or both made back roads impassible for a car. Sometimes they'd be out all day and even half the night, driving thirty or forty miles. Once in awhile they'd turn over in a drift or get the horses down in snow so deep the beasts couldn't even wallow, but not very often. The doctor said that Smithy was the best hand with horses he'd ever seen, and he'd seen a lot of them.

Smithy had a lot of children, we never knew just how many till the twins came along. It was a wild and elemental time at the Blacksmith's house the night the twins came. The sound of drumming hoofs on the night-frozen road was our first hint of trouble. Smithy burst in, dark and wild-eyed. "The Doc is havin' a hell of a time. It's going to be twins. He wants your woman to come right away. He's gotta have a nurse. He'd ought to have known it was going to be twins, hadn't he, Mrs.?"

"Medical ethics," she said, getting her coat.

"I'll wring the ——'s neck, that's what I'll do. They're all dyin' down there. They'll all be dead in the morning."

"There, there," said Kay, getting into the buggy and feeling for a tight handhold. Smithy leapt aboard. He stood up, pulled the reins and cracked his whip. It was more like jet propulsion than anything else I can think of—fierce, dangerous, and much too supernatural to be of this mundane world.

Things were bad down there. One of the twins had been born, and was just about dead. They were premature. The other twin was being born. The doctor had his hands full, more than he could cope with. Mrs. Smithy was very good, and all the children except for Nance, the ten-year-old girl, stayed fast asleep in bed. That was some help.

An hour or so after the second twin had been born, the doctor left. Kay and Smithy stayed up all night trying to keep the two new-borns alive. The first one had got chilled during his first few minutes, and was very low; but the second one was huskier.

In the dim light of the kerosene lamps Smithy kept lugging in wood and fussing with the range, making the room hotter and hotter. Kay was feeling the infant pulses, and every now and then giving them artificial respiration, a bit of whiskey with a medicine dropper, and other stimulants. A curious sympathy grows between two people who have been up all night trying to keep a heart beating, feeling it stop, and start again, watching death come, and go away and come. It was living against dying; it was *here* against *there* as the child breathed out its life and died, and then was stimulated back to life again.

Perhaps it was that bond of life that made Smithy forget his customary dark taciturnity and talk. He told her all about East Wyndam, over near the New Hampshire border, where he had a thriving blacksmith business when he got back from World War I. Teams were plenty in those days. There was a sawmill and a creamery and a gristmill in that little town. Then his lung trouble that he had inherited from the war came on again and he had to spend a year in an Army hospital, while the business slipped away. "I lost my new electric drill and blower, and a lot of other tools, and that set us way back. The town gave me an old schoolhouse, and the neighbors helped me move it, and I got going again. But just about then the town went to pieces. Hood bought out the creamery and let it stand idle. By and by the roof fell in. The gristmill shut down. Everybody owed everybody else.

"A lot of them still owed me when we moved over to this town. We done a good business when we first come here. I used to work all day and late into the night, and I kept a man too. And now what? Everybody around here is slow about paying. Why should I work for them for nothing."

By and by daylight came. The other children woke up and began to patter around on the cold floor. One of the twins was alive all right, but the other had died so deep no amount of artificial respiration or whiskey drops could bring it back. And now it was breakfast time just the same.

104

Kay made toast and coffee, put the cereal on and sat the children up to the table. But they were too excited to eat much. Pretty soon they slipped down from the table and meandered over to the other side of the kitchen to watch their father, who wasn't interested much in breakfast either. He was kneeling on the floor with a small oblong wooden box before him and a half a box of tacks spilled out by his knee. With a pair of tin-shears that he'd brought over from the blacksmith shop he was cutting white satin to fit the box.

"It's a blessing the Mrs. is doing well, anyhow," he said. "Good Lord, I never thought I could make a coffin for one of my own. Often done it fer the neighbors, but I had a idea I couldn't do it for myself. Still, I can't see the good of giving that undertaker a fat sum that would feed the kids awhile; and by all the saints and angels it takes something to feed 'em too. 'Course, I get the pension, but with six of us—now it's seven, I most forgot—it don't do nothin' like keepin' us right. Crimus, I wish these had both lived—such cute little kids they looked together there in the basket. Somehow I'm not so interested in the one that's left. But I guess she'll be nice, like this fat little devil here." As he spoke he cuddled the four-year-old to him.

Then he went on talking and draping the old hardwood box, while Kay washed baby clothes at a tin tub.

"You know, I used to have funny ideas about death and dyin', but after you've buried two or three hundred men, it stands to reason you don't feel anything about it. It does something to ya. I felt sick in the stomach over in France when we had to dig a big trench and bury 'em, crowds of 'em, chuck 'em in like sticks of wood. But it does something to ya. I never care anything about the dead any more. They're just dead, that's all."

He patted the knotty curls of the four-year-old who had climbed up on his back while he squatted by the coffin. She began to clamor for a "piggyback, Daddy."

"And now," he went on, "the blank blank doctor charges

double—double because it was twins. I been driving him with my horses all winter on his back-road calls. And now he says I still owe him eight dollars. All winter! And they're good horses, let me tell you, and they can *move*. Blooded trotters, sired by champions, both of 'em. Only yesterday I drove him forty miles, most of it mud. He made four calls and got forty dollars for it, and he chalked up ten for me. Many's the time we been out all night, no sleep, but I didn't care. I like drivin' my horses. But it's hard on 'em. Comin' home from Hainsville one night in February they was down in the snow a dozen times. They broke the harness all to pieces, and the cutter turned over twice. But I got him home, I always got him home. I thought I had him all paid for this baby case. He told me I did himself. Now he's changed his mind. It was twins, so I owe him eight dollars more. He won't get it, that's sure."

The youngest, a two-year-old boy, was walking around the kitchen in a pair of wet pajamas, munching out of a box of puffed wheat, barefoot, humming to himself. Half the puffed wheat grains slipped out of his fist and got strewn around the floor, and then he walked on them. The oldest boy, nine, was wandering around behind him with a sharp hunting knife, whittling on a softwood stick, and the shavings mingled with the puffed wheat. They both seemed to be pretty good at avoiding the tacks, though nobody spoke to them about it. The blacksmith even plucked a shaving out of the coffin, but there was no reprimand. He was telling about a racehorse he used to own.

Kay carried in a breakfast tray to the mother, followed closely by the puffed wheat boy. Mother looked quite well, though untidy. The child put his dirty hands on the dirty counterpane, and she smiled, patting his knotty curls. "They are a handful, aren't they?" she said. "But they keep well, and that's a blessing."

"Yes, it's a blessing," said Kay. "You know, Mrs. Harris, you should have had some prenatal care, and then the other twin might have lived too."

"Yes," she answered, "people ought to have a lot of things."

Back in the kitchen the blacksmith hammered a tack emphatically. The box was nearly finished, covered outside, lid and all, its inside padded with cotton wool and lined with the satin. Cutting a last small piece with the gigantic tin-shears, he said, "This was my wife's wedding dress. She had to cut into it last year to make Nancy a dress for the school concert. Hated like hell to do it too, but she would have hated worse not to be able to fix the kid up some kind of a rig to sing in. Awful cute Nancy looked."

Nancy, pretty, ten years old, stood by with wondering eyes, watching the last touches to the box. "Are you going to put the little baby in there, Dad? The little dead one? Gee, she'll look nice in there, won't she? Are you going to put 'er in now?"

"Yes, I'm going up and get her now." He mounted the stairs and returned with his bundle. "There, how's that?"

The children gathered round, smiling, happy. The two-year-old's pudgy fingers left their imprint on the white satin. "She looks dandy in there," Nancy said. "Couldn't we put the other one in too, they look so cute together?"

"No, no," he said. "Beat it, run along. Here, Nance, go to the store and take the kids and get 'em an apple and a orange apiece."

They trooped out, and he glared at Kay savagely, as though she mightn't approve.

"Better a rose to the living than a wreath to the dead," she reassured him.

"Damn right," he said, and nailed up the lid.

For about two weeks the smith's team kept the mud churned up between his house and ours. Every day he'd come up and get Kay to go and see to his wife for a couple of hours and then drive her home again. She said it was a wonderful ride except for the mud in the face.

After awhile she went only every other day and then not at all. We didn't see much of the metal worker till one evening along about suppertime he came trotting up along the road in his two-horse buggy, pulled up with a flourish in the middle of the muddy front lawn (cutting deep ruts) and while the horses danced holes in the grass he reached in the back and pulled out a big long bundle of raspberry canes.

"Everything all right down at your house?" Kay said.

"Sure," he answered. He stood up in the buggy and flung the raspberry canes down onto the grass. "There! Don't say I never paid you! You said you wanted some raspberry bushes. All right. I dug the whole damn lot of 'em out of my garden. Burnt most of 'em. They was spreading all over hell. I'm glad to get rid of the blasted God-damn' things."

"Thank you," said Kay.

"Don't say I never paid you, now!"

"I didn't ask you to pay me, and you know it."

"Well, I've paid you anyhow." With that he deftly wheeled his team and galloped back down the road, his horses' flying hoofs throwing mud twenty feet into the air.

We planted the raspberry roots in one long row and they thrived. They were a particularly succulent variety, big and red and flavorsome. Nobody knew the exact brand name—we called them Rocky Reds, just for fun. Somebody had had them from somebody who had had them from somebody, and so it went, about four generations back. We ate bowls and bowls of raspberries with heavy cream, on summer mornings when the dew was sparkling like diamonds, and the morning was still cool, almost cold. To have more raspberries heaped in the big bowl on the red-checked tablecloth than a family of five could eat (we had two boys and a girl now) seemed the crowning glory of our place and our living here. One of those intangibles that's worth about $6,000 on a summer morning.

The raspberry roots spread each year, and we divided them and set out more till we had nearly half an acre of them. There's something about this soil that seems to be just right for raspberries.

They were our greatest luxury—one of the few fruits that seem to thrive with little care in this icy climate. All in all we got more out of that bundle of raspberries than we ever would have from a hundred dollars cash.

And although this seems like almost enough history, there was more to it. For three years during World War II the blacksmith went off to work in the Brooklyn Navy Yard shops. He's a metal working craftsman of the kind they were scouring the nation for, and they paid him big money, naturally. But the family found life there in a tenement pretty cramping for the six children in comparison with the brook and the fields and the lake and the woods. The wife said, "The longshoremen who lived near us were nothing but brutes. They ate and slept, and in their off time did nothing but drink raw whiskey and curse."

The war was no sooner over than back they came, all excited about life in the country again, all excited about fixing up their house, plowing their garden, building fences for a couple of cows. "No life for a human being down there," said the blacksmith. He borrowed a machine cement mixer, got his boys all to helping him, and put a new cement floor in the blacksmith shop. He built the whole thing over, added a second-floor carpenter shop, got himself an electric welder for repairing trucks, and immediately began doing quite a business fixing everything from leaky milk cans to old sleighs. First thing you know up he comes to our place and says, "You know, my wife wishes she had some raspberries in her garden."

So we gave him a bundle of extra roots, and now he has a row of them growing right where they were before.

"We're the keepers of the flame," said Kay that evening. "Come on, let's run out to the raspberries. We've just time before dark. You know, they're immortal, they're much more important than we are. I'm never going to worry about anything as long as I live."

19

THE STORIES and books weren't selling too well that year, so I took a job as teacher in the local high school, known as the Academy. The reason for the name academy was that in the early days the tough old settlers had no school so they founded one and paid for it out of their own pockets, which made it a private school, or academy. Long since, it had become a public school, but kept its proud name. I had never taught before to any extent, but, considering the family bank account, it seemed a good time to begin. The school was two-and-a-half miles away. I taught first- and second-year French, first- and second-year Latin, and Freshman and Senior English. I taught five classes each day and managed the study hall during a sixth period. I became faculty advisor for the Senior Class, organized a school paper, which I had to edit the most glaring errors out of, and coached a hockey team. This latter was a pleasure because I like to skate, but before we could begin I had to boss the building of a rink in a natural swamp at the edge of some woods near the school. What with milking cows, splitting wood, studying like mad, correcting the usual snowstorms of English papers, and getting to and from school, it kept me pretty busy.

I don't think teaching is very much fun. It is fun to see the new idea sprout, of course, and fun to be and work with youngsters, and there's nothing more worthwhile. The chief trouble is that teachers are always so insanely overworked and underpaid that you feel like something of a sucker as well as a Samaritan. In New England you are expected to be a pillar of the community when you teach, and the community thinks it owns you. I knew a girl who was teaching in one of the towns west of us, and she used to go to her home town every weekend, fifteen miles from there. The school board had already told her where she could board and where she couldn't—which is to say they gave her the choice of boarding with the sister of a school board member or not having the job. Now they gently informed her that since she received her money in the school town, she ought to stay there weekends and spend her money where she earned it. She compromised the matter by going home every other weekend, and they threatened to fire her, but didn't.

I ran into it in a dozen ways and had to make it plain I wasn't going to work Saturdays or vacations very much. Teachers were not supposed to smoke because it was a bad example for the boys. So I smoked whenever I felt like it. The boys were down back of the horse barn smoking like mad every noon hour and everybody knew it. I proposed letting them smoke around the outside of the school instead, but it was a couple of years too early for that.

The teachers I met were the best part of it. We used to close up shop and go off to teachers' conventions about twice a year, and there I'd meet the people who were carrying the loads. Some of those girl teachers in the little one-room schools were doing such a job as the pioneer women themselves. Many a little school had no water within a quarter of a mile, and a boy or girl would be selected to go and get some in a bucket. Some boy got a dollar a week or so to come early and light up the big heater stove each morning. Half the pupils came in rubber boots, than which there is nothing colder for making the toes ache. Some of those girl teachers were getting under twenty dollars a week and spending five or more of that on stuff for the kids—supplies, special storybooks, candy and favors and crepe paper for parties and suchlike. They were always getting up plays and sociables at the school

111

to raise money for improvements such as electricity or a new chimney. I was proud to be associated with such people.

At the conventions we sat in auditoriums listening to inspirational speeches on the subject of Education with a capital E. We were told that we were indeed carrying the torch of learning, that Democracy depended on us, and that the future of America was in our hands. The speakers were nearly all superintendents who, in order to get more money and less work, had climbed onto the shoulders of teachers and were now exhorting them to greater efforts. I knew a wonderful old hard, wise widow-woman teacher who, after a particularly didactic oration, jerked her thumb at the orator and said, "Those who can, do, you know. And those who can't, teach. But those who can't teach, teach teachers." Each speech droned on to its clumsily contrived end, and after we had inspected the textbook publishers' displays of new arithmetics and civics books, the meeting broke up. Then it was time for me to go home and milk my cows and spend another evening boning up on Caesar's godamn Gallic wars. I did help subsequently, however, to found one of the first AFL teachers' union chapters in the state.

The daily five-mile round trip to and from the Academy was, oddly enough, the best part of it. It wasn't possible to use the car, because our road wasn't plowed that year. Instead, it was rolled with a great big wooden snow roller drawn by four horses. Seeing the roller go by was one of the great events of our lives—the frosty-maned horses lost in swirling snow; the creak and jangle of the rig, and high on the great roller Carleton Pike with a fistful of lines in his mitten and a look on his face like Napoleon at Austerlitz.

The roller made a good track for sleighs and log teams but would not hold up a car. I know because I tried it and always found that the old Buick, which could punch through two feet of light snow, became hopelessly bogged on the roller track. When the snow really got deep and the winter grew very cold, I used

112

to make the trip on skis. Kim went with me a little way, as far as the Mill Village one-room school, he on his short skis, I on my longer ones. We had knapsacks for our books and lunches, and good parka hoods with a bit of fur around the face for the twenty- and thirty-below mornings. Nothing much showed but his little red button nose, and his breath coming out in clouds. He loved to ski, even though the sun was hardly up, and never seemed to mind the cold. The rolled road made fine slipping to the Mill Village, where he left me—a little bit suddenly, because nobody else's father skied. I cut across the fields toward the church spire on the hill, and I was thinking the North is very fine, with the bright snow sparkling in the low sun, and the deep green spruces and firs. On every side were the clear rolling fields and the great dark islands of trees, not too much of one or the other but just the right proportions. In summer this country is all landscape paintings whichever way you care to look. In winter it's pictures too, but so different and new you wouldn't recognize the place. In winter the pictures are wilder and whiter, with the cleared fields sloping between the woods and making a ski-land like some- thing out of a dream. I had my own special track kittycorner across the fields and I had my own special gaps in the fences and a fine crossing over a stone wall where the snow had the wall drifted clear out of sight for two solid months. The way was all gently uphill, but in the morning you don't mind.

I used to look forward to the evening, to leaving the fret and endless complications of the school. It would be five o'clock or so and getting dusk when I came out and snapped on my skis. The lift of the below zero air was enough to pick you right off your feet, and the fields were only a couple of hundred feet from the building. There the glide began, in the purple and the quiet, making me think that on a long easy slope when you're happy, skiing is like music.

Sometimes the evening was dim with softly falling snow that muffled and cloaked a secret world and fluffed the ski poles with silence. Sometimes the wind was blowing very cold from the northwest, and then I pulled up my big hood over one whole side of my face and loped along in a kind of gliding run that makes you think you're going ninety miles a minute. But mostly at evening in winter the air is clear and still. The lights in the farm-houses way off across the valley to the east would be coming out yellow in the huge sea of whiteness and dark tree islands. And down at the base of the long slope was our own lake turning purple and pink while the wide sky flamed. Beyond the stone wall the grade increased, so that all I had to do was put my feet together and soar for nearly half a mile, watching the sunset and singing because it was so good. You get so you love your skis and your mittens and your life at times like that.

From the Mill Village it was sometimes fun to go up along the level lake, now frozen three feet thick. But mostly I took the route along the rolling road, where you alternately climb and coast. Over the last knoll the snowy peak of the house roof began to show, and then the bright south window with a long icicle hanging over it, shining blue and silver in the light of our new Aladdin kerosene lamp which I had bought with my princely stipend.

20

SPRING AGAIN. These beautiful days fill us with happiness. This is our first real spring after several false ones. The warm sun, the sweetness in the air, the leaves and blossoms coming out—they mean more to us because of the long winter. Our little girl, Susan, is running over the fields all day long, barefoot and half naked. She laughs and plays with the dog and chases chickens and splashes water in an old tub and sings to herself in her own incomprehensible language that so rarely corresponds with ours. The earth is sending up its old familiar magic, the grass is lush and green where Daisy grazes, ankle deep already. Our neighbors are sowing grain and thinking already of the long hot days of haying to come. Last week was still raw and wintry. Now we have paradise and the green haze on the trees, beside a living blue lake that was white and still only recently. Spring, that old story. I hope I'll never be reasonable enough to resist it, hope I'll always yield to its never-failing, never-realized promise, the grand old fraud. Spring is hope, hope for what? Whether its promise is ever fulfilled depends upon what one hopes for. It promises a few more days like this, a few more whipped cream castles of clouds, a few more blue lakes, a few more hours in the grass while the flies buzz or evening cool and hush come down. Spring promises other springs, other days to melt your heart after long winters when you thought surely this time it had turned to stone forever. That is all it promises. Not money, not crops, not lesiure, not success, whatever that may be, but just another spring next year, and maybe that's enough.

We needed a new roof on the barn. The old split shakes that Uncle Hank had put on the roof and patched and repatched were utterly done. Worn thin and tired, they curled up like clusters of burnt potato chips, and even some of the shingles that had been driven in for patches were worn out themselves. For years it had cost me a pang to hear the rain dripping in on my new hay, and many's the night I had stood in the dark barn floor wondering where to find a comparatively dry corner for a grain bag, knowing there was none. Worst of all was the thought of the grand old frame timbers rotting. Uncle Hank, who had put them there in his young days, hadn't been able to buy a new roof to shield them. Once he had roofed them, and then age caught him. By this time Uncle Hank was a personality to me and a familiar, though he had died a year before we bought the place. I knew from working round the place how he felt about Kow Kare and other veterinary remedies, how he repaired a bucksaw, and a hundred little ins and outs of settler ways. He did not always do things well, but he did them fast, and that was sometimes more important. He had left behind him a pair of sawn maple-wood arches for a new pung, several half-hewn hickory handles, parts of a cherry-wood table, several half-finished neck yokes and dozens of appealing old hand-wrought irons whose use I couldn't figure out. Up in the hay loft, tucked into a dark corner of the plate, under the eaves among the hayseed I found three empty bottles of Painkiller and two of high-alcohol-content vanilla. Perhaps when he was discouraged he solaced himself with those, not letting Aunt Mary know.

I had a feeling I owed it to Uncle Hank to keep the rain out of those big beams so they wouldn't fall and the walls sag out and the roof cave in and the lone rafters point a finger at the sky in the bleak way we had seen so many times—all (like the horseshoe nail that lost the battle) for want of a roof.

116

It took a hundred dollars for a new galvanized roof, and this I procured by taking the usual schoolteacher's summer vacation, namely, a job.

The job was a State Agriculture Extension project that consisted of going round the farms of Cabot and Marshfield Townships getting information on a farm questionnaire. It was late June, the time of lilacs and green-carpet grass that grows inches every day. I had our garden coming well. Lane Kent said we could turn our cow in with his and he'd sell milk to Kay for five cents a quart. I would take the old Buick—it was only thirty miles—and come home for the weekend each Saturday noon. The job would last about a month.

Cabot-Marshfield was one of those smiling green valleys full of hills. You know the kind. Eight of us questionnaire men were installed at the inn, a big white-painted hostelry that rambled all over the landscape and had a flower garden out back. Mrs. Barnet, who ran the place, dished up feasts of peas and pork and mashed potatoes with cream and pies and all such, served by two pretty farmer girls. Every morning at eight we set off in various cars and split up to visit farms separately. The rugged tillers of the soil were not exactly in love with us, since our job was to extract a lot of highly personal information from them as to how much they made and how much work they put in. The investigation was to go for ten years every season, and this was the fourth year, so, fortunately, they weren't entirely unprepared for our official prying. They were all haying for dear life, and we'd trail them round the hayfields asking between forkfuls pitched on the load, "Now, potatoes. How many potatoes did you raise last year?"

"Oh shucks," the farmer would say, "I can't remember. Hell, I dunno. I got no idea. I had five acres in potatoes but I dunno how many bushels."

I soon learned a few of the mean tricks, one of which was to say at this point, "Well, shall we put you down for, say, sixty bushel to the acre?"

117

This usually brought forth a roar. "Sixty bushel! B'god, if I didn't get a hundred and sixty bushel to the acre I'll eat the bags. That's a good piece of land there, and b'god, mister, when I put in a piece of potatoes I aim to get somethin' back. Sixty bushel!"

It was June and the air full of fragrance of flowers and grass. I sat by the roadside under a maple tree waiting for one of the cars to come and pick me up, and I wondered how anybody could be so lucky as to be paid for wandering around the countryside this way. I walked a great deal between farms and over fields, frequently not waiting to be picked up by a car that would carry me to the next farm. Often the road was half a mile long to the next place, and that suited me well. I was not very good at collecting figures and adding, subtracting and dividing them, and there were a thousand things I didn't know or care to know about the farming costs of these people. But I tried not to worry about all that.

After an hour or so most every farmer would get restless and say he couldn't spare any more time. He would usually say, "Come back this evening at milking time." That is if he was polite. Quite often he meant to say, "Get the hell out of here and don't be gumming up a busy man." I didn't blame them much, because the questionnaire was a fulsome thing, four pages long. Some of the farmers who kept good books and were cooperating with the study were able in an evening session to give us pretty complete answers. The best of these men were willing to concede that it paid a farmer to keep books so that he could look back and learn some lessons from his own farm history. They believed in this ten-year survey and understood that ten years of records from many farms in this particular region, giving yields, costs, sales prices, amounts of labor, equipment needed for the planting and harvest, and all that, would prove what crops, processes, size of farm and methods made a profit over the years, and which didn't. It was a treat to make an evening date with such a man, to draw up to his desk in the sitting room and see him get out his spectacles and blank books. In an hour we could button the thing up and teach ourselves something in the process. From such a man we had records from the preceding years and could usually repeat the introductory data concerning the physical plant of the farm: how many acres, rented, owned, how much in cropland, woods, pasture, number of cow stanchions, breed of cows, size of silo, any contagious abortion. From there we went to the crop record, acres, yield per acre, total, how much bought, how much sold, how much fed to the cows in winter, how much in summer, amount and kind of fertilizer used for silage, green feed, small grains, grain hay, mixed hay, clover hay, hay bought standing, hay on shares, potatoes, gardens, etc. We plowed on from there through a page of dairy and livestock records by months and ages: how many bull calves, heifer calves, turkeys, hens, hogs, colts, how many bought, sold, raised. Next a pasture record of numbers of head, date turned out, date taken up in the fall (many of them left their cows out much too late in the fall, and it was plain to see how the milk check dropped off as a result). Following this came the difficult matter of the milk record: how much is used in the farmhouse, how much is sold, and—the most difficult question of all—how much was the milk check, month by month. Reticent New Englanders didn't like to answer that one very much. Our instructions were to do the best we could, and if people would not answer, very well, let them answer what they would and the rest could go. Our boss, Jack Hitchcock, told us that the first year a great many farmers had refused to answer more than five or six questions, but that year by year as they better understood the survey's purpose, they loosened up, until by this the fourth year, there were only a few who were balking.

Page three of the record dealt with feed purchased. This really interested me, for it is an axiom in Vermont that as milk price goes up, the western-raised dairy ration that is so necessary for winter feed goes up too. Also I have often noted that the richest man in most small Vermont dairy towns is the grain merchant.

119

He takes mortgages for grain bills, gradually acquires eight or ten farms and usually winds up as one of the chief directors of the local bank and dies of heart trouble and overeating at sixty-six. Such is success.

With labor records, man-hours on the farm, man-hours working out for cash, day help, month help, trucking, teaming, we hit the home stretch of our terrible four pages. And here too was another ticklish matter, to wit, how much unpaid time do your wife and children put into this family business? It was all in the way you asked the question, quite like picking up a skittish girl. "I s'pose those two boys of yours are old enough to be quite a bit of help?"

"Well, Jesus, I should hope so."

"What do you s'pose it comes to, all in all, just roughly?"

"Wal, Jed brings the cows in from the night pasture and milks a couple. Tom runs the milker now. He's gettin' to be a pretty good teamster, likes horses, he does. Harrows some. Evening milkin'. They're all the help I've got for hayin'."

"Say—three hours a day, average?"

"Yeah, say three hours."

"Each?"

"Yeah, each."

And so a little figure of 2,190 hours goes into a little box on the mimeographed record sheet.

"Now do you mind giving me a rough idea of the time your wife puts in on the kitchen garden?"

"Say an hour a day, summers."

Even when the wife worked in the hayfields most of the summer, which was rare, they wouldn't put it down. They didn't like to admit that daughters liked riding hayrakes either. Woman's place is in the kitchen.

"And you, how many hours a day do you average?"

"Oh, about fourteen."

It was like walking on eggs.

In the evening the record takers gathered at the long table at the inn, stowing away Mrs. Barnet's feasts and exchanging adventures of the day. Somebody had been today to see Fanny Smith, the old school teacher who lived and farmed alone, and this year she had consented to answer five questions, which was a great victory for agricultural science.

"What did she say after the fifth question, Jack?"

"She said, 'Young man, I been mindin' my own business for sixty years, and you better do the same. Good day.'"

The town was full of characters, naturally. There was Link Armory, runner-up for the state checker championship, who kept a set of checkers in the cowstable, another in the hay barn and three in the house. If you wanted any records out of him, you had to play a game of checkers first, and that wasn't such a hardship, because he could trim the daylights out of you in about seven minutes.

Four of the men had been on this job before, and they had a great advantage and were able to get more records in a shorter space of time than the rest of us, because people recognized them and accepted them.

"You know Herman Mallers, down by the creek? Went today and he was pitching on hay in the lower field. He said, 'Crimus, you here again? Tell you what I'll do. If you'll pitch hay for an hour I'll get out my books and answer your questions for an hour. Do ya good to earn your dinner for once.'"

"Did you?"

"Sure. He had his hired man on the rack, and him and me pitching on from both sides. We went through the field on a full gallop and mowed away three loads in sixty-one minutes. Then he fed me doughnuts and root beer and we did the whole record in two hours."

There were families that moved every year and got nowhere. There were families on rich farms that had taken four generations to make, who were cashing in at last. There were men deep in debt who thought we were a sheriff's posse and had half a mind to shoot us. There were jolly ones and sour ones, but they were almost without exception very busily haying right now and tremendously overworked. The old ways of brute toil—people have very largely forgotten such ways in the cities. Here was nothing else—physical, outdoors toil that bronzes you and burns you and makes you lean and hard, toil till you get your second wind and work on and on and on in an atmosphere of perpetual, accustomed weariness that finally results in tremendous endurance or breakdown. Early in the mornings, at five o'clock, the mowers in the dewy fields began to chatter. We were having an unprecedented streak of fine weather, and they were all trying to profit by it. Late at night in the cowbarns the lights still burned where they were finishing up evening chores.

We had to leave our supper every evening and go out to the farms again to catch the difficult parties at their milking, finish up records or even begin new ones. "Nothing like a fine evening's rest on the milkin' stool," said a nice old fellow to me. He had been all day in the hayfield, and he now had eighteen cows to milk by hand. When I leaned against the cowshed wall and got my back all covered with whitewash, it pleased him no end. I was glad to have pleased him, and felt that if I could so easily provide him with relaxation, I'd be glad to do it. There was another farmer who was studying to be worshipful master of a Masonic lodge. He had a book full of stuff to memorize, so he tied a string around the middle and a weight to the other end of the string. That way he could hang the whole business over a cow's rump and study while he milked.

In the mornings many a man would be surly at first and refuse to give me anything. "I got no time." With such a person it was necessary to hang on and keep trying. I walked beside the wagon and remarked on the sleekness of a mare. I said, "That looks like a new harness on the mare too." When he paused, I paused. By and by he began to get used to me. "You doin' this all over town?" said the farmer.

122

"Yes, they've given me their records at the places on each side of you. All records are confidential, no one is going to be told how much you make or why you make it or anything like that. This is a study of averages, to show that if a hundred farmers make money doing a thing in a certain way, that must be the profitable way to do it."

"You know a hell of a lot about farming, likely. Book farmin'."

"No, I don't know very much about farming. Not half as much as you. I'm just beginning to catch on. I was born in a city."

"Oh, city feller, eh?" Disdaining me, he speaks to the team. "Giddap."

The wagon travels slowly. It is not hard to walk alongside, though a little hard on the pride. The wagon stops. "You see that mare?" says the farmer.

"Yes, I see her."

"Paid fifty dollars for her, and she's worth three hundred as she stands. Homer Longman, you know him?"

"No."

"He thought he'd skinned hell out of me when he traded me that mare. Come and tried to git 'er back last month. I says, 'Homer—'"

Follows a long tale of horse trading while the sun climbs in the sky. This is followed by remarks concerning Guernseys versus Jerseys. The man gets down from the load and we sit in the shade of a hedgerow. He tells me about the time his barn burned, and how his wife got sick and is now at White River Junction hospital. He tells me how he came to farm this farm, and about his father who owned it, sold it, and bought it back again. We go to the house, where he gets lunch and we eat together. He tells me about his son who ran away, about a book he read last week, about the Cabot town meeting last March. For six solid hours the man talks, almost without stop, about his relatives, his friends and enemies, his philosophy, his aims, dreams, despairs, failures, the history of this farm of his—which is tangled up in a dozen lives, of course.

123

Finally I get some records from him, and it is only by being firm almost to the point of rudeness that I can beat down his insistence that I stay for supper.

I go back to the inn, along the dirt road, under the tree shadows, through the sharp and beautiful scents of brookside mint and sprouting clover, down the hills, around the bends, to the green valley meadows. My colleagues at the inn are fine fellows: extension experts, high school agriculture teachers, graduates of agriculture colleges. A good bunch with their feet on the ground. But after a day with talkative Mr. Waldo Billingsly, my colleagues' passion for translating life and sorrow, earth, sky, family, struggle, craftsmanship and birth into averages to the third decimal point doesn't suit me very well. What we have wonderful rows about is their passion for mathematics and applied science. They *believe* in mathematics, whereas I *disbelieve*. And my disbelief is as active as their belief. They claim that dollars and cents is efficiency, and I claim it is not. The way I make them maddest is to submit the proposition that maybe a forked stick is more efficient than a tractor, and maybe tractor plows will shorten our civilization by five thousand years.

One of the record-takers was a blond-haired fellow named Snelling. He wore glasses and was from Wisconsin, not that the two are synonymous. But he knew a good deal about farming, and, having worked at this job for six weeks the previous spring, he was quite familiar with the farmers and the ways and means. He was kind enough to help me in many ways with the intricacies of filling out the forms, and often of a morning we would leave Mrs. Barnet's fine collection of flapjacks, bacon, baked potatoes and pie, and set off together to work adjacent farms. As well as being a student of agriculture, he knew a lot about rural schools. It developed that he was in somewhat reduced circumstances, and had spent the preceding winter selling stationery and school supplies. To this meager line he had added a few textbooks along toward spring, but obviously business wasn't brisk. He was no salesman anyhow, but he had a family to support.

Ordinarily rather shy, he was talkative too. Walking along country roads between farms with me, he often opened up and told me about buckwheat or the history of land use in China or the salient features of different kinds of clover, or how to balloon frame a barn. Once when we were sitting under a maple tree by the roadside waiting for one of our cars to pick us up he even told me about himself.

He and his wife had been coeds together at the University of Wisconsin. Both of New England extraction, they had always hankered to have a farm in Vermont; and not to just have it but to work it themselves. It was more than a hankering. It was a way of life that they craved. They craved it enough to suffer years for it, both before and after. When they got out of college they both worked and scrimped and saved, and when the depression struck, they had enough to put down a thousand dollars on a Vermont farm and move in, with something left over for tools and such. The farm they picked was way up in Sarksboro in the wildest ruggedest part of the state. They bought a team of horses and eighteen cows, and they really dove into the farming business head over heels.

"I didn't realize," said Snelling, "at the time I bought my stock, that, helpful and kind as our neighbors were, it's a tradition that no holds are barred in a horse trade or a cow swap either. I'd always known that swapping is a sharp business, but the neighbors had been bringing us cakes and telling us where to lay out the kitchen garden and we'd all been figuring out how we could improve the schools there and so on. The horses were sound enough, but ugly. If I didn't work 'em hard every day, I could hardly manage them. They'd been spoiled when they were broken, likely. I used to work about eighteen hours a day, plowing, harrowing, milking, working out in winter. Marge worked like a galley slave too. The first cows we bought wouldn't breed, or got mastitis or had something wrong, every one of 'em, and we had to trade them all off and get some

125

more. That set us way back. Milk was low and we began to get in debt pretty deep. Finally the horses ran away and wrecked a manure spreader and stove me up so I was in the hospital three months, and that finished us."

They had lost everything, really everything by the failure of their farm. And it is not pretty when a husbandman must go out on the road selling crepe paper to the tight-fisted spinsters who run novelty shops.

"What kind of work do you think you'll go into now?" I said.

He smiled kind of sheepishly. "What I'd really like would be to go to farming."

On a hilltop farm at the end of a lane one breezy day by a milk-house door I met a burly fellow with a red face. Before I could open my trap he said, "What're you snoopin' around here for?"

I explained for the umpteenth time the survey business.

"You been to my brother's and he sent you up here to find out about me, didn't he?"

"No, I haven't seen anybody else with your name."

He knotted up his great arm. "B'god, if I ever catch him up here, I'll break his God-damn neck. I don't have no people spyin' around my place." He looked at me calculatingly and rubbed the stubble on his chin. He held open the milkhouse door. He narrowed his eyes to slits. It was cool inside, but dark. "Come in here," he said, standing behind me with his thick thighs just touching me and his telephone-pole arms cutting off the view.

I entered, thinking how sad it would be to disappear without trace.

He sat down heavily on the cement curb of the milk cooler, into which was piped cool water that poured from a spring. I was tense and determined. A quick blow on the head was his plan, perhaps; then into the cooler with the body.

"Sit here," he said, and reaching into the water, pulled out a pint of rye. "Have a drink."

We each had a swig. "Every time I go to town," he said, "I get in a fight. I don't go no more. My brother, Jesus, how I hate that bastard. I like to killed him last time I got drunk. The only way for me is to stay up here on the farm and not go to town."

We had another drink and lit up cigarettes. "It is rather nice here," I said.

"Yes, it's a pretty good farm. I'm going to raise me three dozen hogs this year. I'm going to raise me a lot of young stock. I'm not going to sell no more whole milk. I had a fight with the milk inspector too, the ——! I'm going to sell cream and raise young stock on the skim milk like my father done."

The records poured out in record time and we parted the best of friends, only mildly tipsy by this time. Once again I had a job to get away without hearing the family history for the last hundred and fifty years.

When we could get an evening off, Snelling and I liked to go down to the Cabot Creamery and look in the big stone building where the cheeses were stored. I took a ten-pound one home every couple of weeks. Thousands of big round ones stood on the shelves in that cool structure, and every day or so men turned the cheeses a bit to make them ripen uniformly. Wonderful cheese it is, orange and nippy and luscious, and the Cabot cheese, as well as Cabot butter, are famous in that part of the state. The creamery itself was full of the most modern steam can washers, pasteurizers (they don't pasteurize their cheese, you may be sure), self-recording vat scales, electric separators, belt conveyors and testing laboratories.

It's nice to see a local project truly going, not fake, not defunct, a small local enterprise truly grinding out the grist of democracy. Rare enough it is, too. Most everywhere you go you see only the remnants and ruins of the thrifty old days of local industry and local independence. Cape Cod, Maine, Vermont, New Hampshire, it's all the same; gone, gone, only the old days and the summer visitors to talk about the charm of the antique remnants of a vanished independence. Centralization wins. Sold out to bigness that claims to be efficient and is not—that is what remains.

I do not believe we can buck the trend to bigness in many lines. Autos, railroads, plastics, textiles, they are all pretty big and must be. But a man will still always be a man. I know too that new forms of littleness within bigness have got to be worked out—the littleness of individual men, such as me, to have scope within the larger frame. And if this cannot be done, what good is it all?

My hardest case was Olin Smith, who to date had always refused to give any information to government sycophants. "We might as well try him again," said Jack. "Just call on him, that's all."

I encountered Mr. Smith in the barnyard, a long-jawed man with graying hair and those bright blue eyes that nothing ever seems to tarnish. He had on a woolen cap, though the day was moderately warm."

"How do you do, Mr. Smith."

"How do."

"My name is Merrick. We're around taking the Cabot-Marshfield farm records again."

"Oh, one of them government fellows."

I commenced my spiel about the values of the survey, but it was no use.

"We don't need the federal government around here wasting our time and our money telling us how to farm," Mr. Smith informed me.

"We are only trying to find out, scientifically, which crops and methods—"

"Now you listen to me," said Mr. Smith, putting his foot up on a fence rail in an argumentative way. "What good are these damned records except to provide fellows like you with a soft job at the taxpayer's expense, just tell me that."

I'd had a bad day and didn't care, so I said, "It's not such a soft job when we meet people like you, Mr. Smith."

128

For some reason this touched him, and he took his foot down off the rail. "Hm." He stuck his hands in his pockets. "Tell you what I'll do. Come around at chore time and while I'm milking I'll tell you what I can."

So I got some records from him that evening and met his wife and kids. He was one of the best farmers in the valley, and you could tell from the way he handled his barefoot boys and his heifers that he was the soul of kindliness. The soft mild sounds filled the cowstable: the cow tongues lapping grain in the mangers, the whisper of hay, the milk jets frothing in the silvery buckets. The bright-eyed little boys peeked at me from around the dusty corners of the barn, and it was wonderfully sociable the way they giggled. Papa wasn't having anybody tramp on his toes, and for that I don't blame him. He was overworked half to death, and he was one of those rare individuals who take it out on strangers instead of on their families.

The investigation will go on for years and all be translated to punch card systems and run through infinities of calculations via electric machines. But that means nothing to me. The conclusions of the investigation as far as I'm concerned are as follows: There are at present two men in the Cabot-Marshfield area who love farming and get joy from it. Neither farms for his complete living. One is an insurance man with a fifteen-acre place. He has fruit trees, two cows, grapes, berries, a big garden, a horse, and a nice little barn that he built himself. He took me around his place with a species of pride and affection and a feeling for growing things that I hadn't seen anywhere else. He grows things because he likes to grow things, and he never once spoke of the price they would fetch at a market, because he merely eats them. Very simple.

And the other one who loves farming is Snelling. So there you have it.

21

WHEN I HAVE BEEN AWAY from home and returned and know that I can stay and savor things, I always go and get acquainted with the lake again. One must have time, time to dream and look down through the water if one is to know even so small a lake as this. Lying there against its shores of rock or field, it is so varied in color and mood it almost seems to have a personality and life of its own. It is blue on summer mornings and gray when mist is falling. It sleeps and glares on sizzling summer noons, and then again gnashes its teeth with suds and streaks of foam. Stars mirror themselves and wriggle in the passing canoe wake. In the fall it is cold and black and glassy, with curled leaf boats sailing sadly here and there, not going anywhere much.

We have our special places, of course: the bank on the far shore where a cold spring runs in just above the lake surface; the low shores where grizzled ageless cedars lean over so far you can sit on their trunks and dip your toes; the cliffs where birches and firs stand at the edge; the reed grass swamp at the far end where wild ducks make their nests; the lily pads that are the frogs' special province; the gray rock ledge points; the willow shores; and the place where our pasture grass runs green to the very water. The lily pad patches are special, where the old bullfrogs sleep and open their eyes and blink. It is wonderful fun to sneak up on them and catch them in our hands; even more fun to let them go and see them streaking down through the water, the great legs kicking and gliding, kicking and gliding. Three brooks run in at various places, each of them totally different in its way, and there is one "secret" cove that doubles back inside the shore and runs into the shadowy woods in a way that always surprises and fascinates us so that we have to follow it, speaking in whispers, and then we sometimes smack the water with a paddle and shout. The bottom has its variations, with shallows, deep holes and rock ledges that wind here and there. In the night when you suddenly touch one of those underwater ledges with a paddle blade, you feel as though a monster is rising under you and you get a sense of vertical dizziness that is quite different from the horizontal kind. The two islands are, of course, special kingdoms of their own. On one is a fireplace spot and a diving rock. The other is long, and thick with brush, where, under a cliff, in a subsurface cave, the muskrats live.

When I came home from Cabot, I embraced the lake again, and swam in it and drifted on it and listened to it again. When the kids were in bed, Kay and I took the canoe and went paddling out into the darkness. There were no stars, and the thunder was rolling over the mountain to the west. So dark and still it was, the canoe seemed lost and we moved without seeming to move into the deeper shadow of overhanging trees. We kept looking over the water to the house to be sure that all was safe there in the warm hush that seemed to have grown suddenly dangerous.

We paddled home across the inky water in the ominous heat and stillness of the coming storm. Crickets were singing loud, and as we slid in to our own cove the willow leaves fluttered faintly. A few tinkling wavelets lapped the rocks and then lay still in an electric calm that held no rest. We hardly spoke as we ran up the hill, our bare feet finding the path in the cold night-wet grass. Lightning lit the clouds as we slipped into the woodshed. We were snug in bed when the house rocked and the panes rattled under the down-drumming hose-blast of the storm. I lay and listened to it roaring on the roof, and it was then for the hundredth time that I was repaid for the re-shingling job, for the chimney flashings, for every penny and nail and for every cold hour up there with Chester. Rachel Field, like so many millions of others, has lain and listened to the rain on the roof. Listen to this:

O lovely rain, fall on the sea,
Silver on silver, liquidly.
Darken each trunk and knotted root,
Give every twig a crystal fruit
To hold, and let the bending grass
Be thick with berries clear as glass.
Film the fierce green of juniper.
Let spruces drip with quicksilver.
O lovely, multitudinous rain,
Knock on my door and windowpane;
Stream through the dark, and while I sleep
Your grave and timeless rhythms keep;

An unusual number of deer were around in the woods that year. We wondered whether it was an increase of the deer crop, or a migration from other sections of the state where deer are harder pressed and there are fewer wild lands, rough lands, rugged lands. Do you ever think, even as deer would think if they could, how man's activities have reversed the world's values? Where are the garden spots now? They are the wastelands, the untillable, the faraway and very cold or very hot, the spots that were not worth despoiling and fighting over. The lush spots, the most favored, are battlegrounds or mile upon mile of farms without character, and in odd ways the best has become the worst. Consider the eastern seaboard cities for instance—Boston, Providence, New York, Philadelphia, Baltimore. They were the garden spots: access to the sea, deep water, fertile land to the shore, that wonderful combination of the land's and the sea's products right at the door. Each of them was a snug deep harbor; each, in its alluvial plenty, lay at the gateway of a river road into the land. If you were a settler, with the eyes of a settler, you would look at the green island of Manhattan and the scores of waterways around it and the great blue river, and you would say, "Of all places on this coast that's where I'll build my cabin." Many did. Very many. And now it is the least suitable for human habitation of any spot on the coast. The best has become the worst, and if you were to pitch your tent by the harborside of Providence or Baltimore, by the stinking water, would you not pine for Alaska, the Amazon or the most difficult areas of the Rocky Mountains? Even our ideas of scenery have been reversed. Most beautiful used to be a fresh water stream, flat fertile land, grass, flowers and the possibilities of food, living, loving, easy travel. Now beauty is a place like Yosemite, or barren mountains, mile-deep canyons, killing deserts, sterile sand coasts, unscalable peaks and cliffs of rock. As Francis Bacon says, if all men were to go crazy in the same way, who would know it?

The deer know it, and so they come to Horseshoe. We saw many of them that summer. One afternoon we saw a doe and fawn swimming across the lake toward our shore. They came out on the field below the house and rested, nibbling on the alders by the water. The fawn was leggy and small, and the swim had taken the gimp out of him. We kept very quiet and watched the two of them sidle diagonally up our back hill. At a barb-wire fence that cuts our field the mother threw up her head, sniffed, saw us, and took alarm. Lightly she sprang the fence and bobbed up the hill, away from the house. The tired fawn followed, just clearing the fence, grazing his hooves on the top strand as he scrambled over. He was scared now, and so was the doe. Bounding up the hill, making for the woods beyond our road, they came to another fence by the roadside. The doe sailed over and disappeared down the road like a streak of light. It made us draw our breath and almost cheer to see that effortless leap. The tired little fawn paused at this second fence; there was a ditch beyond it, and life was so difficult. The children wrung their hands to think how he would get scratched on the wire. But suddenly, with a funny little wriggle he ducked his head, folded his knobby legs and slid under.

We were so surprised at that downward opposite-of-jump we could not speak. And then it struck us we had seen one of those rare natural jokes that are so funny you almost die. The children laughed till they rolled on the ground. "Oh Mother," giggled Sue, "that funny little deer, he didn't feel like jumping, did he? Oh, ho, ho," and they went off into another fit that about finished us. We had heard of jokes in the folklore of animals but never seen one before.

Often we discovered their hoofprints in the pasture that year, and now and then in a woodland pasture we came on deer browsing with the young stock that were turned out for the summer.

When our garden began to get nibbled off and the beans and spinach tops were mowed a little more each night, we were still convinced it was woodchucks because we'd had a lot of trouble with woodchucks before and shot at least a dozen of them. Kay said she wasn't going to have the beastly woodchucks ruining *our* garden, so she got up early at daylight, put an old coat over her nightie, took the loaded .22 rifle, a rug to lie on, and stole out in the dew to hide between the rows and fix the morning marauder so he'd never maraud any more.

When I was lighting the kitchen stove an hour or two later, she came in smiling. We had heard no shot and been wondering about her. "I was lying there almost asleep," she said. "It's lovely in the dew in the morning. But kind of early. All of a sudden I knew there was something behind me. I turned and looked right into the eyes of a big buck. He wasn't ten feet from me. I don't know how he got there."

"You were asleep."

"I was not. Anyway, I blinked my eyes and he took off. Gee, I couldn't have shot him for anything—the prettiest sight in the world. You know the roadside fence. He soared over that and the roadside and ditch beyond, made two steps in the middle of the road, then took off again over the fence on the other side. It was fifteen feet if it was an inch, that last jump. I expected to see him sprout wings."

That's the way when it comes to deer hunting. They seem too pretty to hunt. Everybody else hunts deer in season around here as if it were a religion. "Been deer hunting yet?" they say, and I feel queer to be answering no. A whole bunch of men go off south to West River every fall and have a wonderful three-day junket. They've asked me too, but the thought of woods full of game-getters from Springfield, Boston, Hartford, Brattleboro, and East Dorchester takes the edge off it for me. Those down-country birds hunt half the time in cars, scouring the country roads for sign of a track crossing a road. If there is new snow, the deer have a bad time of it. Six or eight hunters will band together to take turns on the track, night and day to wear the deer down. If the track is running easterly, for instance, they get out their maps and figure where it may cross a road. Then, while one follows the trail, other drive to the possible crossing and wait for the deer or the hunter. Of course there are plenty of man-shootings, with so many determined venison procurers in the woods, each with his manhood to prove. I know a fellow who crossed a clearing and heard a voice say, "I had a bead on you all the way across," and many are the near-misses and holes in hats. One of the southern Vermont papers printed a little story one year: DEER HAVE GOOD SEASON, SIX HUNTERS SHOT, FOUR WOUNDED, SEVEN LOST. I remember asking Ethan Cutler, who is a great hunter, if he ever thought of the possibility of getting plugged by a stonecutter or spindle winder during deer season, but he merely sniffed at that. "If anybody takes a shot at me," he said, "he better shoot straight the first time. I'll kill him if I can see him. I was up back of Albany one time, it was late afternoon, when somebody across the other side of a little thick valley took me for a deer and clipped a branch right over my head. I moved behind a tree and fired for the puff of smoke. Then I lit out round the end of that valley to try and run the critter down. I looked everywhere, but he got away."

Such is deer hunting. I know that if a certain number of deer were not shot each season the deer population would outgrow the feed, and an equal or greater number would die of starvation. All the same, when the deer go by lashed limp to the enamel and chromium of fenders and bumpers, I'm glad they don't belong to me.

22

THE WILD DUCKS come again each fall, and always their coming has a poignancy sharp as knives. At sunset when the sky looks cold and the fires of the west are streaked with dun rags, they straggle in from the north and pitch on the waters of this little lake. In the shadow of the firs they feed and sleep, bobbing on the wavelets. In the starlight still I can hear them, a quarrelsome one squawking. Are there some who rest and feed there in the darkness in a panic? When they fly by day so fast, so far across the sky, are there some who lag and sprint? Travel is so ruthless, the weak so defenseless. Travel is so ruthless to find out the weak muscle, the malformed bone. Not today perhaps and not tomorrow, but after weeks and weeks. The sinew that grows weak instead of strong with use. What does the leader say in the long days when the laggards lag? Do ducks have a leader anyway? Do they remember these ponds and lakes from year to year? Of course they do.

Always at the end of summer when the nights grow cold, the ducks come flying in. And I see them and wonder why I am alive.

Sometimes along about Thanksgiving, after a freezing and thawing period, the water on the lake ice freezes glassy. The whole thing is polished, and for a few weeks then before the big snows all life centers around the lake ice.

Every afternoon after school there are hockey games, with Saturdays quite a crowd skimming in and out among the islands. Down by the Mill Village a bright fire burns, where you can sit on a log and toast your toes, and the scene resembles Currier and Ives, except that it's a little less studied. Kids of all shapes and sizes dart around, running and sliding if they have no skates. More than half of them have none, but they run about cheerfully just the same, buoyed by the thought that someday they'll get a set of blades; or maybe even right away brother will lend his. Some have sleds which they run and slam on. Now and then their brothers will pull them for a fast zip around a big circle, and the little fellow sits on backwards, a blissful smile curling his mouth, till his brother dumps him off and bangs his head.

Always, winding in and out through the zigzagging tag players, one sees the child with a skate in his hand—a key skate, a clamp skate, that will not stay on. It tears off shoe heels and grinds a sole to pulp but will not stay fastened. At last the child throws it on the bank and goes off one-footed.

We have a homemade sled with a huge sheet for squaresail, rigged on a pole mast and crossyard, and aboard this contraption we fly before the wind, runners rattling and everybody laughing. Getting back upwind is something else, with a long rope to pull on and everybody howling "The Song of the Volga Boatmen." When we get tired of pulling, we take the rope and use it for playing snap the whip.

The hockey game goes on, with crooked sticks, a block of wood for a puck, stones for goal posts, till we are all so exhausted we can't stand up. Then we lie flat and kick our heel points into the ice and look at the sky and steam. The boys did not know much about hockey till I showed them, but they take to it very readily. It is good for them to know more about offside and teamwork. At dusk they say, "Tomorrow, hey?" and nod their heads enthusiastically and go off home to help with the milking, feet thudding on the frozen ground, skates jangling over their shoulders. They are good kids, salt of the earth, good stock, fine examples of the

138

fact that if you can't have perfection, it is better for a child to have too little than too much. And they know work. Perhaps they know it too well. A man ought to spend full time teaching them games and camping tricks and the techniques of profitless happiness. The light in their eyes is quite something.

Most everybody skis in our town nowadays, though it was practically an unknown art in our earliest years. For such a snowy land, where the skating ice is soon covered and the drifts lie deep five or six months, the skis are truly wings, making an asset of what used to be a long and dreary season. The roads were the only paths in former days, except for an occasional snowshoeing hunter. But now the pole-pocked ribbons streak off everywhere, and even a few dairy farmers will clamp their rubber boots into the harness and try it with the children on Sunday afternoons.

Our old friend Swami—a wizard on the boards as a result of his schooling years in the Swiss Alps—taught most of the local boys how to ride the snow. He got up ski clubs and school meets, cross-country races and slaloms, and for those who couldn't buy skis he made pairs and gave them away. The school kids took to it, and particularly favored slaloms down through sheer-sided maple sugar places where the "flags" were tree trunks two feet thick. Many and wonderful were the homemade ski rigs in those early years, and the most wonderful of all belonged to Wilton Shay.

On the regular Sunday afternoon ski-bees below the cemetery he'd be whizzing through the trees like an old stager, the tails of his big brother's ulster flapping far behind. He was about four feet high and the coat was three-and-a-half. For ski boots he had old rubber knee-length boots with an axe-cut in the toe and a red inner-tube patch stuck on. One of his old pine ski points was split half off, and the tail of the other was laced together with wire. His toe clamps were made of pieces of bent-up band-iron, hack-sawed off a wagon body, and his heel straps were nothing but canning-jar rubbers. For poles he had two broomsticks with can lids for rings, and as mittens he wore an old pair of socks. He surmounted all this with a French toque and tassel that streamed in the wind, and when the pack took off, jostling one another, down "Hell Bent Gulch," they had to go wide open to keep with Wilton.

From below we were watching one afternoon as he thundered down through, making faultless high speed turns in rapid succession between the trees. At the bottom he fell. A highschool girl slid by, and he began to mutter. Picking himself up, he said to us, "Cripers! Girls! I can't ski when there's girls around."

Sometimes on winter nights of deep snow and full moon it is so unearthly blue outside that sleep is impossible. The long icicles hanging from the eaves gleam in the moonshine and the shadows of the trees lie soft and purple, with every twig outlined and motionless. I take my skis from the woodshed and snap them on. The long boards whisper in the diamond powder. Everyone is asleep, lights out in all the farmhouses, but the world of hills is alive with wonder, and the faint sigh now and then from the sprucetops only deepens the certainty of real-unreal.

The smooth swoop to the lake is like being winged, in air so still the cold feels warm. *Pick, tick* go the steel-shod poles on the ice below the snow. The stars twinkle above dark firs that ring the lake, listening. The hills around the horizon are almost as clear and blue as in daylight, but farther away and more mysterious. In a dark blue patch of woods way up the valley a fox barks and the sound dies away with a lingering ring over the lonely ridges.

Up through the woods, across a pasture the skis take me and down the long glide of a slope where the violet track unrolls like a double ribbon. On sharp turns the snow flies up in a crescent of silver dust and slowly sifts downward like motes in the sunshine, but rainbow-wise, with golden shine mixed into the settling curtain of silver. Sometimes I fall, and lie in the fluff, as warm as in a nest, watching the stars twinkle. Everything is dry, nothing sticks, only the leathers squeak a little.

The moon travels its long arc across the sky, and I go on, unable, it seems, to tire in the winey air. The way winds through a sugar woods like a park, but as the maples thicken and the aisles crowd in, it becomes a cathedral, all verticals of barred purple, stately somehow, against the diamond floor. What makes it a dream maze is that the purple tree shadows are heavier than the moonbeam tree trunks. Seen from a bare hill, the countryside dreams in the snow with unique gentleness. In summer the land is always busy, grass blowing, leaves a-flutter, water winking, and the contrasting shades of green and gold speaking of endless growth. Now the land is a lady who likes to sleep, head half buried in the pillow, no stir of foot, only a faint smile, dreaming. It is as though now at last you might hear the earth breathing, though there is no sound.

A push of the poles sends me gliding down through a fence-gap and among pine aisles and sloping glades, faster and faster to the brink of a steep pasture that is misty with silver. The hollows and lumps are hard to see in the uniform sheen of moonlight, and I go crouched to absorb the bumps as the pace increases and the tears stand in my eyes. But suddenly, at the brink of the steep pasture, soaring too fast, I slide off the invisible lip of a sheer drift into mid-air. Good Lord! Who knows how high that wind-cut, drift-cliff may have been or how far below in the shadowless glare the snow will turn solid again? For a long moment I crouch, a painful and contrite hollowness inside, and advance one foot in the faint hope it may save my neck, then land with a shock, plummeting downward, wobbly but upright by some sixteenth miracle.

This is too much magic for me, and I swing a short turn and stop in a shower of silver. Climbing up to the drift wall, I see it is a sheer nine-foot drop that I wouldn't take off from in daylight on a bet.

The spell seems broken by a kind of homespun joviality, and I go home by the rolling road past the half-buried farmhouses, dodging the friendly clumps of horse manure and the wisps of redtop and timothy blown from hay sleds that have been carrying fodder from one barn to another.

It's great to slide into one's bed and think of all the days and hills tomorrow and tomorrow.

Once or twice a winter we go to Mansfield if we can manage it, to see the crowds. Some wear Alpine hats with feathers and have bare knees. They are tall and short and grim and gay, and on the practice slope by the rope tow they are so crowded on a "good" day that it is common to see fast ones clattering across the ski ends of slow ones with a sound somewhat like a train clattering over a switch. The slow ones don't like it much.

Hundreds, perhaps thousands, of the girls and men ski with unbelievable skill and grace. There are dogteams from the Inn giving rides for $5 an hour, and Swiss and Austrian ski champs giving lessons for $10 an hour. In the classes for beginners are fat old ladies and middle-aged stenographers, glamour girls, mama's girls, high school boys, and contractors, the quick to learn and the slow, all executing the same maneuvers, in the manner of classes. It is a revelation in kinesthetics to see the lithe instructor demonstrate a snowplow and simple turn. It is so easy and graceful, he is half asleep. Next in line to try it is Mrs. O'Grady. Bump, bang, she comes down on the wide seat of her ski pants with a crash that shakes the mountain. By and by the instructor gets so bored he shoves off down the steepest slope he can find, doing wonderful turns and geländesprungs and one-foot acrobatics and bowknots. You can tell the Swiss and Austrians a long way off when they are climbing, by a certain different thrust of their shoulders that Americans seldom use.

Chromium ski poles and homemades—there's endless variety brought in by the ski trains that fill the town of Stowe till every farmhouse bulges and people are even sleeping in haylofts. Some have thrilling times, and some have lost the knack, you feel. Once, on the practice slope we watched a beautiful girl in sky-blue tailored ski slacks and shining jacket piped in white. She had aluminum poles, handmade boots, laminated, steel-edged skis, and red mitts trimmed with white fur that looked like ermine. Quite pitifully she stood there alone in the crowd all afternoon and took only three hesitant steps.

Once, by the gateway to the chair lift that runs up the mountain I stood in line next to a man from Maryland. He was an *aficionado*, very tough and fond of the hair-raising, down-mountain run called the Chin Clip. He was stamping his foot and swearing at the delay. "When there's no crowd to wait for," he told me, "I can make seven runs down the mountain in one day. But today I'll be lucky to get in four."

"Don't your knees get shaky?" I asked him.

"Sure," he said, "but you only live once."

A time or two I've been on the mountaintop at sunset when everyone was gone. The sun sinks behind the Adirondack ranges of New York State, and the bays and broad reaches of Lake Champlain ice turn pink, saffron, and violet between the points and islands. It is arctic there on the crest, among the wind-scooped snow shapes that lie ten and fifteen feet deep. The little dwarfed spruces on the upper slopes are buried and crushed under cones of ice, their branches pressed tight to their sides. On the wind comes a cold so sharp and knifelike one cannot face it. The night comes down with a gentle caress and savage whip-cut combined, and something of elemental time and space pour from the sky, giving a pure objectivity and detachment. Men are so small and unimportant they get lost in a sky as big as this. Only to be part of the night and the mountaintop—that is what counts. What does one care for the silly human heat and food needs and all the other needs, now that darkness is coming and the valleys are filling up. For once, one is free and bodiless in the wind, even at the same time that a fur hood against one's cheek and remembrance of the dimness of the waiting descent all make the objectivity intensely subjective.

On such an evening I once started down the Teardrop Trail on

143

the west side, though the Teardrop is too difficult for me. That has always been the least-used side of the mountain, and I like it best. There was no sound but the wind and the skis. The snow holds light a long time, and the dusk was still bright enough for me to see that a skier who went off the edge of the rampart-like turns would land in treetops 200 feet below. Besides that, an icy, breaking crust increased the chances of a twisted ankle, and that would have been very silly up there alone. I snowplowed and did Christie zig-zags, or turned uphill, or sat on my paired ski poles which served as brakes; as a last resort on the extra sharp turns I subsided stern foremost into the drifts in the manner of Mrs. O'Grady. The farmhouse lights came out in the lowlands, and the trees grew black. It was something grand to remember. It was pleasant too to know there'd be no sudden cry from behind, "Track! Track!" and poles thwacking trees and a wild clatter like railroad trains going through switches.

23

VACATIONISTS are variously known in these parts as summer folks, rich bugs, or campers. None of them camp, and some of them live in veritable mansions, but they're campers just the same. Many and various are the stories about these queer creatures, and since we are outlanders but winter folks, we are in the curious and vulnerable position of hearing from the farmers how odd the summer folks are and from the summer folks how odd the farmers are. Both parties think the Merricks are queer as can be, so it's all even.

Twelve miles from us, by the shores of Caspian Lake, locally known as Greensboro Pond, there is a hive of summer activity. Two thousand "campers" move into their lakeside cottages every July and August, to disappear again at Labor Day. Many of them are college profs and teachers. A number are ministers. Dean Christian Gauss made it originally something of a Princeton colony, though the Bliss Perrys of Harvard were there quite early too. There is a unity and a character to the summer inhabitants, just as there is to the winter folks. It bears no resemblance to the shifty namelessness of the incoming and outgoing streams of money spenders in Florida or Atlantic City. These people come every summer for generations. Their children learn to swim in the lake, first come alive in these hills and valleys, have their favorite picnic spots and rocks and hilltops and mountain climbs and blueberry lands and dirt road hikes in this beloved summer homeland. At

145

fourteen and sixteen their boys get strong in the hayfields working for some farmer who often becomes a lifelong friend. Some of the college profs are old men now, and they return in the warm summer days to the old family cottage, crowded with sons and daughters and grandchildren. And the old boy shows his grandchildren the favorite rocky coves and hidden glens, and the upland pastures where the Green Mountain chain looks best against the sky. The older grandchildren roar around the crooked lake roads in beach wagons, telescoping most effectively now and then. But something of the old entity and oneness and character of them all goes on, nevertheless, and it is nice whatever it is.

You should see the elder summer folks at Greensboro handling the local artisans—plumbers, carpenters, masons and such—trying to get them to put up a new garage or install a new bathroom over the coming winter. They do not treat plumber Grudge like visiting royalty, because Mr. Grudge doesn't like to be fawned on. Neither do they slap him on the back in easy fashion, because Mr. Grudge doesn't like that either. They wouldn't think of ordering him or condescending to him, because that, of course, would be fatal. They handle him with kid gloves, without seeming to. They make a few suggestions, quite casually. It is a thing of understatement, and of considerable uncertainty at first.

"What about a new bathroom for us this winter, Joe, on the back there beside the kitchen?"

"Well, I tell you, Perfessor, I haven't got much time this winter. Got twenty cows to milk, and five or six jobs over to East Hardcastle. My wife ain't well."

It is necessary to talk for a long time about Mrs. Grudge's sciatica, and you'd better not try to minimize it either.

"Maybe in the spring then?"

"Maybe."

"How much do you suppose it will cost?"

"Oh I won't rob you, Perfessor. We won't fight over that."

146

Probably the bathroom will be there the following July when the Professor's clan gathers again. It isn't any use drawing up any very detailed plans. The more detailed the blueprints are and the fancier the architect, the more the Greensboro carpenters and plumbers will improve on them and vary them. They are craftsmen; they do fine work and they insist on scope for their own originality. They are always putting in closets and handy gadgets where they don't belong, but by and by people get used to the innovation and say, "You know I'm very glad Mr. Hobson put that closet in there."

A favorite Greensboro yarn—and rather more of a favorite with the summer folks than with the winter folks—is the one about a Greensboro plute who wanted to order some fireplace wood, but made the serious error of neglecting preliminary amenities. He tramped up onto the porch of Johnny Black's farmhouse one day and thumped on the door. When Johnny, in his socks, came trailing out, the plute let fly without a second's warning, "Morning, Mr. Black, I want to order some firewood."

"Too bad," said Johnny. "I don't take orders from anybody," and gently closed the door.

Another standing joke in Greensboro is the diametrically opposed taste of winter and summer folk. Farm people lay hardwood floors over old wide-board floors to cover up the cracks. They plug up all old fireplaces and plaster them over, because fireplaces leak air in winter. They cover old hewn ceiling beams with plasterboard to make a smooth and dust-free ceiling. When summer folks buy an old farmhouse, they do just the opposite—rip up floors to expose old broad boards, open up fireplaces, expose ceiling beams and even chip them if they aren't chipped. Winter and summer folks laugh about this. "We ought to just trade houses," they say.

Many of the summer houses have two and three bathrooms. Most of the farmhouses have one bath, but some have none. I do not notice much envy on the part of poor Vermonters, however, for summer riches. When the great exodus rolls around, when Labor Day comes and the poor summer folks must leave their true homeland and go and drudge again at lathe and rostrum and pulpit, the farmers feel a bit relieved, to be sure. But the farmers also feel a little sorry for the poor devils.

24

WHEN YOU LIVE in the country you have to expect to have more visitors than you did in the city. It's more fun, too. For whom? That's the art of it.

It got so that a great many people were coming to see us in the summertime. We were glad to have them stop by, but we'd have been gladder in the winter. In summer there has come to be an artist under every bush in Vermont, from which stems the great outdoor sport of rooting them out and running them down. The greatest influx occurred in August in the midst of haying, canning, gardening, and all the preparations for winter crammed into a short summer. They came by car, motorcycle, by bicycle, bus, and afoot, and they sat in the shade while the work went undone, and told us how they envied us our simple life.

Usually the men liked it better than the women, I noticed. They relaxed in the sun and took it all in quietly. Occasionally they lent a hand with the haying or gardening or ditch digging or painting or whatever was going on. In the evening we often sat under the apple tree above the lake and sang and had wonderful talks. We were proud of our little place, and it bucked us up to have people admire it. No doubt we were largely responsible ourselves for the tidal wave of visitors, because it gave us such pleasure to show them our garden and canned goods and cow and lake and house. That it all had value in their eyes made it even more precious to us. We just overdid it, that was the trouble.

I noticed that about the second day, when George or Findley or Ned or whoever he was began to really fall in love with the life, wifie usually had to say, "But, Ned, you wouldn't like the long winters very much, and I'm sure that the wood stoves and no electric refrigerator would soon get you."

"Yes, dear."

"And we have the children's schooling to think of."

"Yes, dear."

She was too tactful to mention the outhouse and no running water.

Perhaps the trouble was that most everybody spent a night or two and we were already up to the ears in work. It got so bad we even made up fables about it, one of which went like this:

Once upon a time there was a small man named Horace Small and his wife, Louise, who lived way up in the New England mountains and wrote books. They were not very bright, but they got on okay until a lot of people started coming to see them to find out what life in the country was like, and after that everything went to pot.

It made Horace jumpy. "What's that!" he said. *That* coming up the road and craning its collective neck turned out to be Aunt Ella's nephew, Willoughby, and his sharp friend, Artie Tope. They were on their way to Salt Lake City after a binge in Denver and "just thought they'd drop in" for several days to recuperate. Willoughby was done up in a skin-tight Chesterfield with derby and pointed patent leather shoes. Any farm family would have run him through the corn sheller at the age of three.

"Boy, have you got a swell place here," he said. "This'll do us a lot of good, eh, Tope?"

"Yeah," said Tope. "Tell me, Horace, have you got any bicarbonate of soda?"

"No," said Horace, "but I've got a few cows to milk."

So they all trooped into the barn.

"Jeeze, how much milk does a cow give, huh?" said Tope. "What, this one doesn't give any, huh? She's 'dry' eh? Well, I'm dry, too. Say, Horace, you mean to say you haven't got any liquor around here? Man oh man, this is worse than being lost in Central Park. Well, she's 'dry' huh. What's she dry for, as you call it?"

"She's going to have a calf."

"Oho!" He lowered his voice. "So she's *that* way, huh? Jeeze, Willough, come 'ere, look, she's *expecting*. The stork, you know— a little stranger. Isn't it sweet? Gosh, Horace, what's the other one kickin' at the pail for? Why, she's standing in the milk. Gosh, she's kicked it over, gosh I wouldn't want to drink it now, what'd she kick it over for, Horace?"

"On account of your making so much noise," said Horace. "They won't stand for yapping the way humans will. Scram!"

"There, you see!" said Tope, walking away. "*You* don't know about animals, Willough, like I do. We haven't been socially introduced, see? And the expectant mother, of course, has very strong likes and dislikes, in her condition, and she just doesn't like *you*, that's all. Com'mon, there's a pretty birch and I need a piece to write a letter. I gotta prove I been to the wilds."

One week twenty-nine people came. Going to the Gaspé. On the way to Chicago. "Just dropped in to say hello."

"Four hundred miles out of the way to say hello?" asked Louise.

"Oh well, the car is new and needed breaking in anyway."

Hoeing corn in his overalls, Horace told one lot of semi-strangers that Mr. Small had gone away. "I'm his hired man. He left word he wouldn't be back for six months. Gone to Hawaii to see about pineapples."

Another batch rolled up and hollered, "Am I on the road to the Small Farm?"

"No, no," said Horace. "You're dead wrong. You turn around and go three miles back to the crossroad. Take your left and your next right. The road's pretty rough, sort of like a cowpath, but keep going. It's over that far ridge there."

151

"Thank you very much."

"You're welcome," said Horace.

Girls with cameras showed up; also a long-haired gent peddling his own poetry in home-bound volumes, hand-printed in green ink, hailing Horace as "Brother Author." Delegations of women from the Honest Toilers Association requested a speech at next Thursday night's sociable.

Unknown relatives were troublesome, but total strangers were worse. "Can you tell me where this road goes? By the way, Horace Small lives here, doesn't he? I happen to have a book of yours here. I wonder if you'd mind autographing it for me. Nice little place you've got here. Let's look around, dear. This is my wife, Mr. Small—Mrs. J. Harbeak Grosspatch, Mr. Small. And these are my two daughters, Millie and Sillie, we call her, and Sulina's husband, Vennie. We had to leave the little grandchild home. We said to ourselves, Mr. Small, we simply couldn't pass through this part of the country without stopping to see you, we all admire your—ah— book, 'So Linger Here,'—m-mm, so much."

"No, no, Father, 'No Singing Here.' "

"Well, anyway," said Mr. Grosspatch, "if you'd just put your name right here. Mother, where is that book? Didn't you put it in?"

"I forgot," said Mrs. Grosspatch.

"Well, well, I'm sure a man of Mr. Small's wide knowledge understands what it's like when a big family starts off on an outing. Ha, ha. Don't you know. The confusion and all. I tell you what we better do, Mr. Small. Doubtless you have here a good many copies of your 'No Lingering—,' what is it, Mother?"

" 'No Ringing Cheer,' " prompted Horace.

"Oh yes. Well, I'd suggest you sign one and let us take it, and then we'll mail you ours when we get home."

"I'm sorry," said Horace. "Some people like you were here and got the last copy away from me a month ago, and I haven't had money enough to buy another. And now I must bid you a very good day."

"My friend," said Papa Grosspatch, patting Horace on the shoulder, "you're overtired. We're just going to sit right here on your porch and have a fine folksy chat, aren't we, Mother."

They made for the step, but Louise Small had been watching from the window. She was at the end of her tether. She had broken under the strain. "We're besieged," she had wept the night before. "We live in a regular subway station. It's an active volcano. We're as public as frogs. In the city a *few* people entered or left without barging in on us. But *here* every misfit in fourteen counties makes a beeline for our kitchen."

Now she came running with a shotgun.

"Thanks, dear," said Horace. "Exactly what I need." He cocked the hammer and let go a blast into the air.

The Grosspatches jumped four feet and ran for their car, Mr. Grosspatch screaming, "Hurry, he's homicidal."

Horace sat down on a stone, of which there were many, and Louise cradled her head in his lap. "I haven't felt so good," she said, "since grandpa got his whiskers caught in the separator."

"I know," Horace murmured dreamily. "Isn't it nice."

"Let's fight for our own, shall we, Horace."

"Right you are," said Horace, pride in his brave little wife filling his heart to bursting. "We'll fight it out if it takes all summer, and we'll never let them drive us back to the city."

"I will load for you till I drop," she said simply. "And when the end comes, save the last shot for me."

"Neither friends nor relatives nor darkness of night shall stay our stay here," said Horace, also simply.

So they remodeled their house on the early American lines of the blockhouse, jutting out the corners to give themselves a better field of crossfire. Once Horace caught a luckless uncle trying to get in the second story window and hardly left enough for identification purposes. But it was all right—the dentist had a chart.

They became very good at defending themselves in their blockhouse, and acquired virtually an international reputation for idiocy and mystery. Reporters who couldn't get into the blockhouse circulated ugly rumors about them, and this enabled Horace to dredge up from the bottom of an old trunk all his most pointless stories and sell them to the movies for fabulous sums. And so they lived happily ever after.

By and by the joke began to be on us, and Kay really put her foot down and rebelled. "We have our farm and three little children," she said. "I'm not going to cook and sweep and make butter and fill lamps for a horde of summer transients. If anybody else just 'drops in,' they'd better bring their own bed and breakfast, because they won't get any from me."

After that we evolved a system which worked most successfully. As suppertime and the shades of even approached, we would say to our visitors, "You know, this is wonderful country and you ought to stay around for a few days and explore. There's a grand farmhouse down the road where they cook the best meals! They have running water and electricity, and it's very reasonable, too. They'll give you room and board for five dollars a day. Best meals you ever ate. I'll go down with you and introduce you to the farmer's wife. What do you say?"

That solved the problem. Brains versus brawn. You have to be pretty brainy nowadays if you're not to have a brawny life taken away from you.

Once in a while Duffy and his wife and kids come to see us or we go to see them. They are like us. They live in the country too, about fifty miles south. But with a difference. They do it with a certain elegance because they have an income. They live in a great big house on a hill and have maids and hired men and oceans of books and pictures and visitors and thoroughbred cattle. They also have a lot of ideas. Oddly enough their type of existence and ours each has its advantages, and we find we always have something to exchange in the way of yarns and information.

The Duffys avoid being dilettantes by the fact that they work. Duffy has a mind like a whip and knows enough for ten pepole. He was once a Ph.D. and used to teach at Harvard till the great academic mill began to grind the gizzard out of him. So now he writes poetry, runs a 200-acre farm, milks night and morning, slaves in the hayfield, harrows day and night in the spring, cuts wood, makes maple sugar, thaws frozen pipes; in short, practices all the Vermont arts. His garden is twice as good as ours. He also organizes evening classes in his farm town, has set a bankrupt church on its feet, has improved about 200 per cent the school his children attend, is mixed up in state-wide co-ops, and ten hundred other things. He is studying Arabic and wants to begin making maple furniture if he can ever find time. I suppose the reason why it works so well is that he is always learning. "Damn it," he says, "the only thing I can't manage is my hired men. They work like demons and are always trying to outdo me. It's not that. But they're so touchy I have to tiptoe around about this and foresee that and allow for something else till you'd think I was working for them, instead of they for me."

Harriet Duffy's grandpa was a business baron who cleaned up in the Gay Nineties and at the end of his life, like Rockefeller and Carnegie, began a campaign of contribution instead of acquisition. Harriet's grandpa managed to endow a lot of libraries and things before he died, and to bring up Harriet's father with most of the Spartan virtues, which he passed on to her. She can cook and sew and knit and weave and garden and preserve and ski with the best of them, and withal has a demure sort of charm that is most appealing. The old Romans had a tradition of noblesse oblige and believed that one of the uses of wealth was to bring up children to ride and fight and swim and box and farm and study. All this was mostly for boys, but Harriet's pa included his girls in this old classical ideal and succeeded in making them

155

competent and able to cope. Harriet went to forestry school for a spell and knows a lot about trees. She manages a big tract of woodland in West Roadstone as a kind of a model to show what can be done, and the thing pays for itself in saw logs and firewood and pulpwood. She's pals with all the farm women for miles around and besides raising three children of her own has helped immeasurably to make their town a good place to live. One of the best things she ever did was to spark a down-to-earth campaign aimed at better care for farm mothers. She visited two-thirds of the doctors in the state herself, and like most of the other things she tries, she put it across. They are like us also in that they don't get misty-eyed over mossy old water-wheel mills or care two snaps for the by-gone charm of a vanished era; they like Vermont for what it is right now, this minute. They love its valleys and rocks and hills and weather, and above all its people, who have never sold out to bigness or the dollar chase or the radio chains or anybody else. Because it is itself, they think the region has a far brighter future than most, and they'd like to be part of that future in ways a man can understand and be glad of.

They come to see us in an old Ford roadster and pitch in at haying or cutting wood as though they lived there. We walk and swim and pick up enough ideas from them in a day to last us a month. Once on a fall evening of full moon they drove in and we had them helping us harvest cabbages and pumpkins and squash half the night to save the stuff from a heavy freeze. Then Duffy sat and told us about irrigation in Palestine and what makes Robert Frost tick. It was he who first gave us the story about the Methodist Episcopal minister, Rev. Ebbett, who organized and made successful a parish cooperative store and credit union in Plainfield, Vermont. Perhaps some of the deacons also operated feed or grocery stores. At any rate, as often happens, strong organized opposition to Mr. Ebbett developed in his parish, and a conference with district superintendent and bishop revealed that he would have to accept a transfer to another church and carry on "a conventional church program." He went home, held a family council, and decided it would be better to change his profession than to compromise his convictions. He resigned and stood by the co-op, "the Lord being my helper."

Duffy had a pasture at his place that was so run down it wasn't good for anything. So he and the county agent went to work on it. They left one acre the way it was, but they fertilized the rest and turned in clover three times. Now it grows grass shoulder high, and people come to look at it from miles around.

Once in midwinter when we hadn't been anywhere for a long time, we drove down to see the Duffys in the old Buick. It was a terrific cold spell and that added to the adventure. We were done up in our furs and mittens and sheepskin slippers, with the children wrapped in blankets till only their pink noses stuck out. Because of the icy roads we had on chains that roared and jangled like machine-age sleigh bells. Especially when you go slow in soft snow they tinkle. We had new isinglass in the side curtains, but one was broken already and let in a stream of air that would almost cut through a board. The plate glass window in the back wall of the cloth top had gotten itself smashed by a piece of lumber that summer, as a result of which we had the hole stuffed up with a feed bag full of hay. Once, on the way, we got so cold we had to stop in a restaurant and thaw out for half an hour by the stove.

But at last we were there at the foot of the drive leading up to the beautiful white-pillared house on the hill. We stopped and felt, somehow, like a bunch of greasy gypsies. "That bag of hay in the back," said Kay. It had wisps sticking out of it and looked pretty bad.

"Let's pull it out and go up in style," I said. So we stuffed it in the trunk and rolled up to the front of the house with a flourish.

Duffy and Harriet were there, laughing and glad to see us, amazed that the children could keep so warm in their three layers of blankets. That beautiful rich and tasteful house, the gardens

157

with fountains, wintry now, the arbors, the blue-stoned gravel drive, the Swedish stove, the sumptuous bathrooms, the great long living room with a fire blazing, the lovely modern paintings on the walls, the books—to us it seemed enchanting to be part of a house like this. We touched the smooth and costly woodwork, the mahogany banister, the walnut tables, and realized that at our little boxy house most of the beauty is out in the snow.

There are always people at the Duffys, and this time it was an Englishman named Alec. He had spent two-and-a-half years in the Antarctic studying the blue whale for the British Government and discovered and proved that they would soon be extinct unless they were given better protection. His report was received by the Norwegian and British whaling industries with a notable lack of enthusiasm, and new whaling expeditions were soon outfitted for the blue whale, so he quit his marine biology and joined the Navy in some oceanographic capacity or other. He was now on leave, and where the Duffys had discovered him I can't imagine.

It appeared that the Duffys were also having trouble with stray hordes of transients dropping in. "Since the ski trains started coming to Roadstone," Duffy said, "we can hardly live. First thing Saturday morning, they pile on us in droves. People we haven't seen in fifteen years come barging in the door, shredding the threshold with their boots and shouting, 'God, am I hungry! Duffy, put 'er there, old sock. God, it must be good to see a face way off here. Where's the liquor, Duffy? When do we eat?' Next Saturday in comes another batch, all doing us a favor, mind you. Missionary work for the Duffys. We'll have to go to New York for some peace and quiet winters at this rate.

"I wouldn't mind the skiing hue and cry so much if skiing weren't being changed from a simple, purely individual sport to a formalized code—like the transformation of college football, you know, into a grim business with a whole train of bogus ethics. *We who are about to die salute thee, Caesar!* There's a cross-country ski champ who lives over the mountain and what do you suppose he does? He runs the course all summer, in shorts, carrying his poles. Says it gives him the feel of the turns. It gives me the creeps.

"Couple of weeks ago a big down-mountain race was scheduled at Roadstone. Well, it was icy, glare all over the hills, you could skate on the roads. No matter, the race had to be run. The skier's code, Do or die, preferably die. A lot of racers were hurt. An ambulance was parked at the finish line with its motor running. The ski patrol with toboggans, first-aid kits, and eager faces stood by all over the place. One skier broke an arm, another twisted a knee, but the prize was a lunatic who finished. He came down over the last *schuss* like a bat out of hell, midway down his skis went out from under him, and you could hear the crowd groan. He catapulted across the finish line one horrible ball of mixed-up skis, poles, feet, arms, and heads, going about fifty miles an hour. This was meat for the ski patrol. They picked up the remains and put it on a toboggan. He had a cracked collar bone, a sprained wrist, a gashed forehead, and a broken ankle. Just before they carted him off, he lifted up his head. This was his moment. The skier's code! 'Boy, that was a swell race,' he whispered and sank unconscious."

We walked in the hills following rabbit and deer tracks in the snow, drove the new tractor, looked at the big barns, spent a day sawing circular wood while Harriet and Kay visited a blanket factory, and in the evenings we talked till one o'clock about the Navy, the Pacific, the islands of the Antarctic, and five thousand other things. By the time we bundled up to leave again we felt new and refreshed, and when we returned to our own home sweet home in the snow, it looked pretty good to us.

25

THERE IS NOTHING NEW to be said about water. We are the only ones to whom it is new. Neither of us ever lies in a smooth shiny tub of warm water without thinking, My! My! and remembering the pipes, the ditch, the rocks, the buckets, teams, cement, ice, the old cistern, the hazel stick and fourteen hundred other matters.

It has been said in desert regions of the Near East that "after the passion of love, water rights have caused more trouble than anything else to the human species." Probably this is putting it mildly. We havn't had any trouble with water rights yet, but we've been through most of the other water troubles.

The original water system consisted of a pitcher pump at an iron sink. Back of the sink was a rotten window with the glass falling out of the sash, and the window slightly below the level of the sink's rim so that most of the splatterings flew down onto the window sill where they were out of sight but not entirely out of mind. The sink was a "dry sink," which meant that it had no drain—merely an iron box in which you were intended to stand a dishpan. Aunt Mary had put in some forty years carrying out the dish water and throwing it onto the grass. We never figured exactly how many woman-miles per average year she walked with the dishpan, not being statistically inclined. Mostly she threw it on the roots of a pine tree behind the woodshed. Dishwater is part of the wind's song in our tall pine top.

Water for the pitcher pump was rain water stored in a bowl-shaped cistern dug out of the ground near the back door. Rain spouts led from the eaves troughs down into this smelly thing. The board cover had long rotted away when we arrived, and the hole made a formidable pit-trap not ten feet from the back door. This was the door the Bakers had kept nailed shut, but we didn't care to be nailed in. The first masonry job I ever did consisted of building up the curb of our cistern with rock and cement. I cleaned out the trash and cemented all the cracks, finally painting on clear cement and water to seal the pinholes. Then I cut cedar logs in the swamp, laid them over the cistern top and covered the whole business with a layer of plank and two of board. Our cistern top made us a kind of patio, where we sat shelling beans and looking out across the lake.

My home study course in amateur plumbing began with the renewal of the pitcher pump leathers, and continued for many years, with the place supplying the problems, Sears Roebuck the supplies, and the U.S. Government the instructions.

Water is one of those things that *gets* you, like death and taxes. You can either settle it or it will settle you. I never minded carrying water in buckets until we began to acquire more stock and children, and then I began to think of all the other interesting things I could be doing during the hours spent lugging water.

Since the rainwater supply seemed inadequate for a bathroom, particularly in winter, I set to and built a new outhouse, a fine and fancy one, the third in my growing experience. It was back about fifty feet from the house. All the neighbors marveled. "What do you build it so far away for?" they said. "You wait till winter comes." There was a picture that year in The Catalogue of a mother with her little child battling through snowdrifts nine feet high. It is night and she holds a lantern. Far away through the storm is the little house.

For a while all went well. The pitcher pump worked first rate, and the stove had a hot water reservoir in it. There was plenty of rain, which ran off the roof and drained into the cistern. If the rainwater tasted flat, we had a small spring across the road from the house in a little hollow.

But when winter came, the ground froze deep and humped up around our outdoor cistern bowl, cracking the cement and letting the water run away. Now there was no rain. It was necessary to pry up the trap door, warm things up in there with a lantern, and plaster the cracks. Zack lent me his team, pung, and eight milk cans. I spent a couple of bitter days in January filling the cistern from a spring-fed water trough about a quarter mile away. The water slopped and sheathed me in ice, but it didn't seem so bad, because most everyone was having trouble with water that year, and many farmers' water lines were frozen.

That is a trouble that happens here on many farms. The ground is ledgy. People dig their pipe ditches as deep as they can, using dynamite now and then to cross a ledge, and usually everything is all right if they can get down three-and-a-half feet or so. Under a road or a path where there is much trampling, the frost will go deeper. In a spring-fed swamp the ground never freezes, and six inches is plenty. But comes a bad year like the one I'm speaking of, when the truly terrible black freezes of thirty-five and forty below hit the bare ground after a thorough-going January thaw. Then the frost goes four or five feet deep some places. The faucet at many a house or barn water trough begins to run slower, then drip, then cease. Somewhere, far away in the iron ground the pipe is solid, splitting probably. Often the pipe will split open in a rent thirty feet long, sometimes in six or eight places, sometimes not at all. I remember the celebration at the Phillips' house the following spring on the 17th of May when the spigot at the kitchen sink—open since January—sent a message from the dark earth nearly half a mile away and suddenly began to spout water. Their pipes had thawed without splitting, and their place was functioning again. During all those months Lyman had had to drive his cows and horses down the hill to the spring-fed water trough, in blizzards, snow to the thigh, ice, cold, rain. His cows' milk production fell off because the water was so cold the cows didn't drink enough, and they drank too infrequently also. During those four months he had had to carry every drop that was used in the house. The problem of the house is a small matter, but for a dairy farmer with forty head of stock the loss of barn water is something else again. He has to toil like a galley slave till spring, and his milk check will be diminished.

The same thing happened to our neighbor Sibley, on Chimney Ridge. He is one man alone to work a 250-acre farm, hard pressed by a mortgage, milking thirty-five cows, raising fifteen head of young stock, a team of horses to tend, and his children all small. A neighbor boy told me about it. Sibley walked into the kitchen one morning with a look on his face like a thunder cloud full of lightning.

"What's the matter, Sibley?" asked his wife.

"The God-damned water's froze," said Sibley. He picked up a heavy iron poker and hit the stove a clip with it that bent the poker. "The God-damned water's froze," he repeated, beating the stove with all the strength of his knotty arms.

"We got to use that stove," said his wife. So he went to work on a bent hickory chair instead. He smashed it to kindling wood in the twinkling of an eye, cursing and screaming.

Quietly his wife took the poker from his hand. "We need the chair, too," she said.

He went outside. It was then morning. He did not come back to the house till long after dark, and even after he returned did not speak to anyone for three days. After that he was all right again.

Water gets you. It's inevitable. It got me, too, after running dry in January for the third winter. I decided we'd have dependable running water in the house or know the reason why.

For a time I was going to pump the low spring, across the road from our house, but Lyman told me it was only surface water, a hole in the swamp. The fact that it froze up solid in winter had almost convinced me he was right. To make sure, I dug the spring out deeper and put in an overflow pipe. Sure enough, the spring ran fine all winter, and never froze a particle till a mouse got into the overflow pipe and drowned himself there. But in late summer the spring went very low—below the overflow pipe, which was only an inch above the ground level of the swamp. So in dry times it was to all intents and purposes a hole in the swamp, as Lyman had said. That's the way with water. It isn't one thing or another.

Our spring water was very hard. Soapsuds disappeared in it like ice in a hot sun. It left a greasy ring around every dish and deposited lime in our teakettle an inch thick. Here was another queer phenomenon: on one side of the river in our town all water was soft; on the other, hard as a brick.

Still I kept trying to find a spring—obsessed by the beautiful picture of an ideally watered hill farm that has a springhouse where the butter and homemade root beer stay chilled; the pipe pours downhill by gravity all year long and never freezes; "Forty degrees winter and summer," the farmer proudly says. And in the barnyard in a great brimming trough the cattle push their noses and blow, while the geese flap their wings in the outflow brook. And there is no pump with leathers to be messing around with.

I kept on looking for a spring all over our hillsides in the woods above the house, digging here, probing there, thinking always that I'd bring in a gusher. I couldn't find anything, so I got one of our more distant neighbors to come and try his water witch stunt.

Is it real or is it a self delusion—the water divining that some favored individuals do with a forked hazel stick? There are records of it as far back as the Romans. The scientists will tell you it is nonsense. But I have seen a man hold the forks of a stick as tight in his hands as he could, and when he walked over an underground vein of water the stick trembled and turned down so irresistibly that when he tried to prevent it, the bark peeled off in his hands. I know that there are some people for whom the stick will do

164

nothing, and I am one of them. But others, with an apple, hazel, or willow fork have almost convinced me of remarkable powers. Lyman says that once on a farm where the water supply pipe had been buried so long that nobody could remember where it was, they wanted to dig it up and put in new. Water was still running through it, but the pipe had so filled with rust that the stream was too small. So they got Ernest Larrabie with his apple fork, and Ernest walked back and forth across the hillside and every now and then he'd say, "Drive a stake there." They drove where he told them, till pretty soon the whole crooked line was marked out. They dug, and the pipe was right below the stakes.

One often hears of such things but seldom or never is present. This same Ernest Larrabie walked all over our upper hillside and found nothing. "It has to be running water," Ernest told me, "and you can't always tell just how deep down it is. Some folks won't dig deep enough."

That's another thing. How deep is deep, and who is going to disprove a water witch's thesis when the answer lies twenty feet below solid ledges? Ernest came into our house and had a cup of tea and told us water stories by the yard, but we still had no supply.

It was a choice between the hard spring and the lake, with a pump in either case. Two summers I had had the lake water analyzed by the State Board of Health. As they had pronounced it pure, and it was fine and soft and sudsy, we set to work piping the lake. Nearly a year it took, off and on, to accomplish our great project. This was only one of many projects, such as clearing a good lakeside pasture of alders and young poplars, seeding down all our fields with new clover and redtop that would give us five times the present hay crop, roofing the barn, painting the house white, making four rooms with dormer windows upstairs, renewing the chimney, enlarging the cellar, building a porch. And I liked them all and felt that they were good and that they were a form of saving and when we had them they would be ours and we'd not have to be paying rent or interest or installments on them forever. Some of those projects aren't finished yet, and they aren't always fun to work on. But by the large they are. Often and often they have made me think, Well, if you don't have money, you can use what strength and brains you've got. Many's the night I've come into the kitchen dog-tired and covered with mud, dropped off my overalls and thought to myself, "Well, we're not working for nothing like so many poor devils"—and felt it's grand and very lucky to be able to make a step ahead each day. If you just lay up one brick a day yourself, you'd probably have a new house twice as quick as you would the "efficient" way by earning and saving the money and then hiring masons to do it.

I built a bathroom upstairs, with some help from Chester; bought fixtures from Sears Roebuck and had to have some more help from the local plumber with soldering cast iron waste pipe and putting in a septic tank. Everywhere in the ditches we struck rock, rock, rock. My knuckles were skinned with rock for months. Lyman was blasting some rock for us in a ditch near the house and blew in a window, even though the small charge was covered with straw and boughs and poles. "Deep enough for ye?" he said, as he looked into the smoking ditch, and I told him yes.

We installed a 200-gallon pressure tank and had to take down the stairs and chop away part of the sill to get it into the cellar. That took six men. I had to work at haying with some of them to pay for these jobs, but there are stories in haying. We installed a sink, hot water boiler, stove water back and two set tubs in the kitchen, carefully leading the pipes up through the center of the house so they wouldn't freeze in winter. While we were at it I laid a water line to the barn and a shut-off valve six feet in the ground, with a long handle sticking up through the barn floor. It all seemed very wonderful to us, but whether we would circumvent the all-pervading frost or not was always uppermost in our minds.

Then began the battle of the ditch to the lake. Winter was

166

coming on, and there was not a day to be lost. Over a week we toiled at that, picking out boulders and chiseling ledges, trying to set the pipe four feet below the surface of the ground. Three-fourths of the way down the hill we found a comparatively soft spot where we dug a big hole six feet deep for our pump house. The little pump and air-cooled gasoline engine had already arrived via The Catalogue—a very fine outfit with a brass cylinder in the pump and an engine like a jewel, with a foot pedal for a crank and a one-pint gasoline tank. But at the lake edge I was stumped. I tried by myself to lay the pipes out into the water where the intake would lie on a rock in four feet of water, and so not get frozen in when the ice became thick. There was no one to help me, what with winter coming on and everybody trying to get ready for it on his own place. I found that standing in a drifting boat in a gale of sleet trying to screw together the ends of two 20-foot lengths of pipe is no work for one man. All I was doing was ruining threads, dropping couplings, and freezing myself.

By this time it was November, with the skim ice forming on the coves. That night I had a bright idea. I waited a week until the lake was frozen about two inches thick. Then I walked out on it with my pipes, screwed them together easily on the level floor of ice, arranged them just where they should be. Next I sawed a narrow channel both sides of the pipeline and kicked it into the water. It sank just right with the end strainer lifted off the bottom on the exact rock I had picked. I lay on the ice with my nose in the ice water, peering at it, convinced the world had just witnessed a major stroke of genius.

But there was no time to celebrate the great event. The ditch had to be filled before the earth turned hard as stone, and a pump house had to be arranged somehow. The latter went well, too. I had a practically new and sturdy privy that wasn't going to be used any more. So I knocked the seats out of it, rolled it down the hill, and dropped it in the big hole, where it has served us as a pump house ever since. You'd be surprised how different it looks,

167

sunk in the hillside to the eyes. That was the crowning triumph of all my hydraulic engineering.

Late that November when the little pump engine began to *put put* and the trial run came off, we could hardly believe our eyes to see water running from the kitchen faucet. The crystal stream, the immortal droplets, a running spring (with help) right inside our house!

Late that winter some skiing weekenders came to see us from New York. They were sitting by the stove talking, when Kim took the woman by the hand and drew her into the kitchen. "Look!" he said, turning on the faucet at the sink. "I bet you never saw anything like that."

26

WE STOOD and looked at Lake Champlain, that long jewel between the mountains, so big and blue and familiar and appealing to us. We had grown hungry for it again. Our own lake at home seemed small, and it seemed we did nothing on our farm but work, work. So we had put our old canoe on the old Buick, thrown our tent and gear into the back seat, arranged to farm out the children with Esther Kent at her place for a week, and here we were, actually at the water's edge. It sounds easy, but it had taken three weeks of careful planning, including three days of the usual fence fixing so that our cows and heifer would not get out of the pasture or into the garden. Just as we get hungry for the ocean, we get hungry for Lake Champlain sometimes—to travel on it and soak in it and take risks on it; and to sleep beside it with the sound of ripples in our ears, and to see the thunderstorms walk over it in walls of purple froth, and watch mist rise from the coves in the mornings.

I'm always sorry more people don't understand the joy of knocking about in small boats. Not that I'm any authority on the subject—having navigated mostly in old dories, battered canoes, sprits'l skiffs, and, best of all, an ancient twenty-three-foot keel day-sailer bought second hand from a couple of Swedish carpenters in Bridgeport, Connecticut. You have to have something that will float, of course. But the main joy is leaving the land— shoving out on your own. And I often think it is the coves, shores, beaches, blue water, towns far away, the sunlight and the tinkle at the bow—they are what you're after. And they are as good and enchanting in a twelve-foot skiff as in a fifty-footer, and much less expensive. This is one thing people who raise their eyebrows at "yachting" do not realize: if you cannot have it in an expensive way, you can have it in a cheap way. The water is still the water.

Consider a little boat, a little centerboarder with sail, rudder, tiller, oars, and to go with it a tent, food box, sleeping bag. Say $300 if you make some of it yourself, as you can. In any case it's far less than a car. Saturdays and Sundays you shove off, and fifty feet from land you have dropped off—along with most of your clothes—the headaches, the traffic snarls, the loss of freedom, the pettinesses and frustrations.

Who can say what the wind does to one's spirit or what a night's sleep at anchor, under the stars, with the wavelets lapping, does to one's view of the world. Nothing can go wrong after a night like that, and to lose all one's money would be the most trivial of mishaps, for is the world not of an exquisiteness almost beyond endurance? There is nothing in all this world quite like sailing. Deliberately you go back to early Greek times (with a few of the more magic modern improvements such as a Marconi-rig-bird-wing-on-edge and stainless steel standing rigging) where nature rules and you know she rules and you don't forget it and you don't try to deny it—you just try to be part of it without getting drowned. Perhaps sailing is for me the symbol of the good ancient-primitive and the good modern-technological that we are trying to achieve. You have the ageless water and wind and danger, the physical vigor they require and the primitive delight their moods inspire. You are definitely a savage as you wing along. At the same time you are modern man, with better-tailored sails and rig, lighter, stronger hull, better shaped, of less resistance. And the savage and the modern are not at war; they are reconciled and balanced. Neither are you fighting nature; you are going with her, fitting, adapting to her better than the ancients knew. For once you are not being crushed between the conflicts of the ages, nor at war with yourself. You are just sheering across the old old wind in a modern boat. There is no motor, there's nothing automatic about it, you're on your own to sink or swim, and your skill and your strength are always necessary, and must be developed, and you must always be learning. All that is a necessary part.

Sailing sums up all I mean about using our intelligence to produce sane, brave, generous lives instead of using every ounce of energy to get ahead of some other fellow. It sums up what I mean about picking and choosing among the junk on the trash pile of the Twentieth Century and all the old centuries, and taking the best and leaving the worst.

I suppose that life for Kay and me will be forever changed because of three years we once spent with the part-Eskimo people of Hamilton Inlet, Labrador. What we saw there was an almost unique, unified group of people who sang and worked and died in a way that was harmonized with nature, and they were happy while they were doing it. They were the happiest people we have ever known. Not all of them, of course. Not those who died of T.B. bones. I do not idealize them. They had motorboats, steel needles, rifles, nails, tar paper, even a few squawking battery radios. What they loved most was their hunting and fishing, their lakes, bays, rivers, homes, way of life. I often wondered why they, with so little, were happier than Americans, who have so much; and could only decide that they are closer to the truth. In those days Kay and I used to take off on sixty- and eighty-mile trips in our little double-sail skiff, ostensibly to get the mail every month or so in summer, but really to spend our days on the great blue bay. There were rains and calms and storms and fair winds, and times when we both had to row to round a corner and keep off a lee shore where the surf was rolling. But we'd look at each other sometimes, winging along a couple of miles from land, and be unable to speak, it was so blessed. The sails were more patches than original cloth, the boat was lapstrake and broad and hard to row. Our craft had no centerboard and couldn't go to windward, and she had no rudder either, which forced us to steer with an oar. But what did we care. If a storm blew up or headwinds continued, we went ashore and set up our tent and picked blueberries and slept and read and cooked, for a week if need be, till the breeze blew fair. Time is very necessary, and also very cheap if you live right.

To be on the water, that's what it is, the water with its colors and infinite change. Sea water has a greenish cast if you look at it in a bottle. Lake water is blue. But under cloud shadows or the moon, there is no end to its color. Perhaps it is that water is endlessly moving, never the same. Perhaps it is water's opposite-ness to land, so valuable, so useless, so unchanging. You cannot fence the ocean, or even Lake Champlain. You have to like the waves and ripples for themselves. Since they do not return your love, it has to be a very pure love, characterized by the old saying, "If I love you, what is that to you?"

Water days and water ways put you close to the weather. You watch the clouds and the sky and the changing colors for other reasons than aesthetics. The rising or falling or shifting breeze is of great concern to you, especially when you travel in small cockleshells. When the shore sinks into shadow and the water turns dark blue against the rising whitecaps, you do not view the scene disinterestedly, for usually there is work to be done, the wind's work, the weather's work, into whose hands you have delivered yourself of your own free will. It is not at all like looking at the weather from ashore, where a storm means principally the loss of one's trouser crease. It's all a question whether you *want* to be one with the rain and sunshine or yearn not to be; whether you are of a contemplative nature that is content to sit on the shore and look at the sea, or must dive in. For my part I think the weather's gifts far exceed the weather's pain, but if I had to go out to the Grand Banks in winter, I'm sure I would say quite the reverse. I don't hesitate to admit you can soon get too much of it. But you can get too much of feather beds or rides in planes or Bourbon whisky or any other mortal thing.

On the water you live or die by the weather, you are soaked if it rains, frozen if it's cold, warmed and blessed by the sunshine and silver, one with the natural world, though often fighting it. Man is such a fragile creature, he can't stand much of nature's boisterousness and live to tell of it. But now and then, even for a little, thanks to a good stanch boat, to be one with it . . . or even thanks to an old canoe with a sail, heeling down a lake, as though you were sliding down a tight-rope with beauty and danger on either side. . . . I never walk beside an ocean beach and see the waves curl in without thinking of the days in my teens when we used to try to run the surf in a canoe, my father and I; and the comber curled and the paddles bent and the canoe picked up speed and shot like a bullet for the beach; or veered as the thundering wave broke, leaving us just time to roll into the seaward maelstrom while the craft capsized and spun over and over into the shallows, with sand in her ends and a couple of cracked ribs, like as not. Canoe ribs.

It colors all life ashore to have known days and nights on the water. When the squalls come down the city street, snatching hats and making the skirts swirl, you say to yourself, "They're pulling to the cabin slide, they've got her reefed way down and they're digging out the oil clothes, out there, out there where the storm can knock them down if it wants to." And you feel the tug of the lowered jib as you and the wind wrestle for it. On a night when the house chimney rocks and you gather to the fire, you think of the open sea, where men crawl flat on the decks, from handhold to handhold, not daring to look up at the dark-caverned cliffs of water that hang over them. The fire burns brighter, and you know that love of the sea is absurd. It is love of the boat, the boat that makes life possible on the sea.

The boat is a means to an end. Like a heavy coat in a blizzard, she makes life possible there. And she is art of a lissome, functional kind, refined by centuries of the most searching experience. No wonder people are forever likening them to women. It is no use saying what a boat is. A boat is fun and a boat is joy if you think so, but if you have a tendency to seasickness a boat is a pure and simple curse. Francis Herreshoff, writing "The Common Sense of Yacht Design," is mixed up in art all the time, the balance, the weight, the strength vs. lightness, the speed vs. stability, the beauty vs. stoves and bunks and self-bailing cockpits. Every boat is a mass of mutually exclusive desirabilities, a mass of compromises.

Which brings us at last to our boat, our canoe, one of the greatest compromises in the history of water traffic. We bought her on the Lake Champlain shore for thirty dollars from an old man whose boathouse was falling down. It was a big old house built in the side of a rock cliff, but the builders had never got their claws into the rock, and now the whole thing was oozing over the edge. Formerly he had made a business of renting canoes and repairing them when the renters returned them to him with holes in them. This led to some remarkable development of his carpentry talents, but not much else. "How old is she?" we asked him of the only craft that still had nice lines and was not swaybacked.

"As to that I can't say," he replied. "I bought 'er from a couple of young fellows who were going away to the war in 1916."

Even at that time World War I was quite a long way back. But we had to buy her because we had to get out on the lake that very afternoon. And we've still got her, patched and repatched, veteran of many a stormy voyage.

On this our latest trip we put the canoe in at Ferry Bay, stowed our weathered gray tent aboard, our grub box and axe and blankets, two folding army cots (we were being very luxurious this time), sail and leeboards, and paddled off. The sun was shining and the water was so clear you could see bottom in fifteen feet. We felt so good we were scared we would die of joy.

We always feel uncivilized, going down the lake. We have our food, our beds, our means of locomotion. We are on our own,

174

for covering distance, for the risk of drowning, for poking round the points. It does not matter that there are white cottages with porches, and occasionally people in other boats way off. They do not exist for us except as a slight menace. Sometimes we get out the grub box and the Primus stove and boil up a pot of tea, drifting in the middle of the lake, the paddles laid down, our heads back on the gunnels or load, our feet hanging over. If we want to slip into the lake for a dip, we can crawl aboard again over the ends quite safely, one at a time, for we have practiced, and when the big canoe is loaded she is quite steady. We come ashore on some long white stone beach like the one below the narrows where an abandoned lighthouse sits on a cliff. We come into a secret cove of white sand and fir trees, the shore of a great estate stretching two-and-a-half miles along the shore—posted, of course, with NO TRESPASSING signs that say $200 fine—and there we camp all night in the starlight and paddle off in the morning when the mist is rising from the bays. We go ashore in a little harbor at the foot of a giant mountain on the New York side where there used to be a small colonial iron mine; silence broods by the ruins of a rock-and-timbered dock.

Years ago the steamboats plied Lake Champlain. On the little old four-car ferry that runs (sometimes) between Ferry Bay, Charlotte, Vermont, and Essex, New York, we met an old man once who told us he worked aboard a steamer that went down the lake three times a week, touching at Ticonderoga, Crown Point, Port Henry, Westport, Thompson's Point, Essex, Shelburne, Burlington, Port Kent, in and out to all the little harbors on the New York and Vermont sides, picking up potatoes, apples in barrels, horses for sale, farmers in wagons, letting off and taking on drummers at the small country landings. The steamer even served dinners aboard, in a glassed-in dining saloon. Apples went by freight steamer from the level clay orchards of Addison and Ferrisburg, Vermont, across to the railroad at Plattsburg, New York, and there was much barge traffic from Montreal through the lake to the Hudson and New York. It was a water thoroughfare, a busy place. Once Burlington, Vermont, was the biggest lumber port in the U.S.A., with docks where the barges from Canada brought in the raw planks and baulks for finishing. A few slum children fish from the rotting remnants of those wharves, and that is about all that remains of the busy waterfront. The great water thoroughfare has become a modern desert, incredibly beautiful, lonely, and less civilized than it was sixty years ago. We think it one of the most beautiful sheets of water in the world, and always imagine that if it spread its blueness and sunshine between twin mountain ranges of Europe, it would be very famous. Along the western lake side run the Adirondacks, some very high, like White Face, Marcy, and the jumbled peaks around Placid. Down the eastern or Vermont shore, all the way from the Canadian border to far below the lake's southern tip run the Green Mountains, blue and old and humpy against the sky, fifteen or twenty miles back across the lake plain from the shore. Drifting in a boat, you see the peaks change silhouette—Jay, Mansfield, Camel's Hump—and think of times you've been way up there in the mountains and seen the lake and islands and its huge bays spread like a map. Not so very far back in geologic time this area lay beneath the sea. From the clay of the Champlain valley plains—best farm lands in Vermont— people have dug up old whale bones, people who, perhaps, will never see the ocean. Somehow it is not like other lakes, enclosed, a dead end, a pool. This one joins with the sea at both ends; touches all the world while it lies smiling between the green fields and the mountains. It's the old water highway and the old warpath of nations, and even to me it is a spirit lifter and a path. Most people have such focal points in their lives, I suppose.

So many things have happened along this lake, it would take a book to list them—and some books have, in the dullest possible manner. Ira Allen died on a hay load, driving over the ice from South Hero Island to Burlington. He just quietly passed away, and the horses jogged on along the bushed ice road track till some chance meeting revealed the fact that they had no driver. In wintertime you should see the shanty villages of tiny houses on runners, clustered on the ice, their stove pipes all belching smoke, and an old Ford belonging to a fish buyer jogging along the village ice-street. Off Burlington there are sometimes clusters of as many as ninety shanties, with far out, off the points, five or six belonging to the restless ones who claim the smelt are bigger out there and bite better. At Port Henry on the New York side are villages of miners and their children too, and their wives, who spend half the winter lugging stuff out to their ice communities—rugs, boards, boxes, barrels. It is pleasant to know that the piles of ashes, fish guts, rusty buckets, broken carton shanties, wrecked sleds and odds and ends will all disappear from these ice communities in the spring thaws.

Sometimes when the lake is slick with smooth ice, in the earlier winter before the deep snows, you see the iceboats winging, seventy miles an hour, their runners crooning, and the muffled, bundled, fur-clad crews literally congealing no matter how they dress. With a skate sail out from Burlington you can make it to the lighthouse on Juniper Island in less than twenty minutes—if you can get around the big crack that lies open even in cold weather off the dog-leg shoal.

Once with a high school principal when the ice was slick I went fishing up toward North Hero. We had borrowed a collapsible plywood shanty that folded flat, with hinged corners and a hinged top that you laid on the walls and fastened down with screen door hooks. All this and his son's Flexible Flyer were loaded on the car, together with stove, coal, kindling and the rest of the necessary gear. When we got to the shore of the fishing bay, we loaded our junk on the sled and set out over the ice a mile or so to a very special fishing ground he knew. A fierce wind was blowing when we commenced unfolding our collapsible rig. The wind caught the plywood, the coal bag began to slide away, the sled started moving, and all certainties vanished. We finally got the walls of the shanty up and the odd corners hooked. I was inside this floorless pen and Dan outside, when the wind commenced to carry us off. The ice was slippery, there was nothing to hold onto, Dan couldn't stop us either, and so we sailed along—me yelling bloody murder. He was scraping away with the ice chisel, trying to get a grip somewhere with its blade. But the wind kept blowing and we kept bowling merrily along, revolving slightly, like a slow top. I was getting good and sick of it by the time he handed in the ice chisel. With that I was able to dig into the ice under the sill and pry us to a stop. Then he ran and got an axe and we quickly chopped a hole and froze her down before she should run away with us again.

Winter and summer, it is always something. In the blinding sunshine days of late winter cars ramble here and there all over the lake ice, and the tolls at the two big bridges fall off markedly.

Sieur de Champlain, it is said, you know, here lost a continent for the French. By assisting a band of friendly Indians and firing upon a party of Iroquois, the French lost the Five Nations, the British won the French and Indian War, and France lost America. Sounds a little too neat to be true. But I often wonder where along the lake, at what cove or beach, on what point, under which cliff it was that Champlain introduced the Indians to firearms and the unpleasant excitement of bullets coming at you.

Nobody knows all the battles and famous trips this lake has seen. Indians on the Deerfield Raid paddled this lake, and up the Winooski, up the Mad River, into the Connecticut and down to Massachusetts. Rogers' Rangers on their famous dash to extinguish the red terror on the St. Francis left Crown Point and followed the lake to the swampy banks of Missisquoi Bay.

Ten miles or so out from Burlington are the Four Brothers, the Vanderbilt Islands that nobody seems to know, where seagulls are so thick they drive visitors away. Maybe they know the Vanderbilts and tolerate them.

The relative of a certain Burlington shopkeeper lives aboard an evil old motor barge that crawls the lake. And with the sharp and

178

darksome relative is an equally sharp and darksome wife. They fish, they gather driftwood. They sell stuff second hand—a boat they found adrift, but the painter rope was cut with a sharp knife; a mattress that was drifting, but it shows no mark of water; a bed they found, but where? Many a lakeside cottage has missed a lamp, a few blankets, some chairs and hammocks. The bargeman and his wife know where they went, for the bargeman and his wife are the last of a long line of lake pirates. Though he comes ashore and works sometimes in winter, the bargeman gets restless in the early spring. After the ice goes out, before the summer visitors come, he takes to his roving life on the lake again, collecting old brass, rugs, baby carriages, occasionally an outboard motor, maybe.

Somebody else who roamed the great lake was Mary E. Wilkins Freeman, who wrote that great story, "The Revolt of Mother." She and her husband, who was a Middlebury professor, had an Oldtown sponson canoe with a little bronze centerboard built in amid-ships. In this they sailed and paddled the lake for a week or two each summer, loving it very much. But now they are both dead and their canoe lies rotting in the hayloft of a Panton barn.

Sometimes you see the cruising folk ashore from yachts wandering around in Burlington, brown and free-looking in sun glasses and slacks. I know a man who tied up at Chiotts' dock, looked below and saw a timber jutting out four feet below his keel. "We can't lie here," he said, taking in his warps. "Why not," said his wife, "have you forgotten there is no tide?" "Gee, so I had," he said, and made fast again.

And so we go cruising down the lake and past an island or two I'd like to buy. In place of Indians, the summer boy and girl camp canoes dart here and there, miles from land, though a thunderstorm hovers.

And it isn't the history or the people past or present. It's the lake itself. In storms the waves dash in on the gray old boulders and wash the points of long red rock and gurgle and spout in the cliff caverns. What we like is sand beaches and miles of stones;

179

the hidden harbors and cliffs of deep black depths beside bent-strata rocks that arch and twist into red somersaults; the miles of blue, with a sun that makes you squint, and a fair breeze that bends the mast; the hayfields by the water, and the cows and apple trees; daylight sinking orange behind the Adirondacks; or dawn coming pink from behind the Green Mountain peaks; the tent in a cove where wavelets tinkle all night; stars, cool swims, hot noons; white squalls and glassy calms; always the beauty and danger. All you can do is feel it tingling down your arms and into your mouth and eyes and nostrils like drops of crystal and radishes and salt.

What we like is the bigness and beauty. What we like is the drops falling from the paddles as we swing together in a kind of effortless dance. We have paddled together, Kay and I, so many hundreds of miles, here and in Labrador, that we push along in unison without trying to. But if our stroke happens now and then to fall apart and get separated and independent, that does not matter; we do not believe in making a fetish of things. Kay in the bow, the load in the middle, and I in the stern—so we jog along mile after mile. If a fair breeze comes, we put up the sail and shift the load so we can loll amidships on cushions. We usually cream along within a quarter mile of the crooked shore, so that if we should capsize in a squall, it wouldn't matter very much. I feel that such caution is somewhat reprehensible, but on lazy days it is more fun not to worry.

Features of shore, trees, points, rocks there were that reminded use of our earliest days in the old Coonrod house. As we approached the gray rock ledges, excitement gripped us and that enchanting "recollection in tranquillity" that sometimes shines out like a lighthouse. We landed on the old gray rocks, and went up the huge natural steps past the blackberry canes. Here was the same stillness and content we had known in the long afternoons when we first sat there with our baby. We had to run up through the pig lot and the woods to the old black house. It was just the same, nobody living in it, and had the same black, blank air of staring blindly across the lake at the Adirondacks. It was only a little, and for a short time, with lights in the windows and smoke coming out the chimney and a woodpile in the dooryard, that we had been able to dent that black staring blindness, and now it had returned. It was sad but not too formidable, since we knew how quickly a family could knock that black, blind pose into a cocked hat. We stood on the hill and looked down at the lake and thought of the winters and the ice. We used to love the lake very much in winter too, a great plain of dazzling whiteness in the sun. There would be prisms and reflectors of rough ice standing up like daytime lanterns here and there miles away, sometimes in clusters, sometimes alone; and as the sun walked, the lights went out and others caught ablaze.

Standing above the lake, we remembered so many things. We had a police dog named Mike, with upright ears and the liveliest face, who loved to pull a sled. We had a little homemade sled for Kim to ride in, with a baby-carriage handle, and Mike would pull it all day long, the only trouble being that as you walked behind, Mike almost pulled your arms out. Now and then of a sunny day when the winter wind wasn't too steely we'd bundle Kim up in furs and blankets in the little sled, hitch Mike, and set off for Bolland Manvers' fish shanty—a little dot a mile or two offshore. He would always be so happy to see us. Once coming back ashore at dusk a bad wind blew up, ten or twenty below and really fierce as it swept that great expanse. We pulled the furs close over the baby till only the tip of his nose stuck out, and he went to sleep while we trotted along behind Mike as fast as we could leg it. Kay was sure the baby would freeze, and she kept running alongside and taking off her mitten to feel whether he was still breathing.

I'll never forget how I loved the winter storms on that lake, running through them alone and not worrying, and feeling free. It was mostly in February that the great white oceans of roaring flakes came down in solid weight onto the miles of icy plain, blotting, erasing, isolating it. Usually that was a blessed time to be home, when the drift literally plugged and suffocated nostrils and the cold searched out every buttonhole. But every once in a while after long battles with the manuscripts, the silly words, the interminable paper, it was the great pleasure of life to run the frozen lake in storms,. The great ice boomed and the wind sang, and its wildness and untouchable-ness and strength and savagery and beauty were something I must know and be close to. It is all very close, somehow, to that chase of the unknown, fleet-footed, capricious, dangerous, wild and knowable female by the unappeasable male; only, this was some wilderness Diana the Huntress that no one has ever seen. In the snow, far from shore, half lost except for the wind's direction to go by, I knew that way off there was Westport, in New York State, snug and smug, with lights shining in the modern age. And right side by side with it was the ageless, timeless lake, brutal and beautiful as a jungle, as wild here in the snowstorm as it used to be before Sieur de Champlain ever "discovered" it. And this would go on, always, in the middle of the lake, this wildness, this beauty, unspoiled, unchanging, demanding self-sufficiency of humans or death, in the summer blue and the winter white.

The same sensation has come to me, rocking four or five miles off the town of Burlington and seeing the great cascades of tin cans and broken bottles winking along the steep backside that the city presents to the water—rocking far off and thinking how good it is to be alone, or with one other. And the breeze blows cool and the ripples sparkle and the mountains change their shades from green to blue to mauve. And here it is again, the wild and the civilized side by side, and we in the middle, picking and choosing a little of each.

182

At evening we came ashore on a rocky island, small, with patches of grass and a few trees in the middle. There were sharp ledges just a few feet offshore and we had to wade in and carry the canoe up. A curious current was setting against the island, which seemed inexplicable until we examined the mainland shore and saw that we were directly off the mouth of the Lamoille River. In a niche of rock we built our fire, made tea in the old black kettle, browned some toast, heated up a can of beans, with a bunch of celery and some sweet chocolate to go along with our meal. There was a nice flat place to set the cots, and because the night was clear and the stars were coming out we didn't bother with the tent.

The airplane beacons far off on Snake Mountain and Mount Philo began to sweep the sky. Now that the lake was quiet and dark, the island seemed very remote. A motorboat with red and green sidelights jogged past toward Westport, faint music coming from its radio. It was a day.

27

WE HAD an awful time each fall getting our hog into a pen in the barn when cold weather came. I used to detest it, it was such an idiotic and impossible job and made us feel so inadequate and futile. The hog would be quite a size by fall, and we couldn't drag him, we couldn't drive him and we couldn't coax him. I have seen hogs that people drive here and there with the cows as meek as lambs. But ours were never that kind. They fought and squealed and went in three opposite directions at once. First we'd put a rope on the beast, one around the neck, and about six more half hitches round his barrel belly. Even then he'd squirm out of it if we weren't careful. There is really nothing to get hold of on a fat hog, as you would know if you have tried it.

We tried to coax him with grain, but he immediately got flustered and obstinate. Then we tried to drag him. But he set his legs so wide and firm you might as well try to drag a well-rooted tree. Quite often he'd drag *us* off, while we hung to the line, burning our hands till we came past an apple tree where we could take a turn and bring him up all standing. I remember two years on these horrible annual occasions when we left him thus tethered to a tree while we retired to the house to think the situation over. Times like that you feel that because you didn't happen to be born in the country all is lost and farm life is hopeless. One year we were in such despair as to ways and means of handling the brute that we lured him into a great big wooden box, nailed it up, and rolled him into the barn end over end like a trunk. The distance was about thirty-five feet, and the job took the better part of the day.

It was the following year that old Zack came to our rescue. I asked him how you did it, and he said, "Why sure, I'll show you."

We went quietly into the pen, carrying a big cedar bucket that had a little grain in the bottom. We pried the bars loose so that one side of the pen was open, and then when the hog began to show interest in the grain bucket, Zack clapped it over his nose. Zack kept coming fast and shoving the bucket onto the hog's snout as the hog tried to back out of it. "Grab his tail now," Zack hollered, "and steer him."

I grabbed the curly tail, Zack kept jamming on the bucket, the hog was running madly backwards, I was steering the hard, slippery rump, and so we waltzed into the barn at a pace that left us breathless. The whole procedure went like clockwork, and before the hog knew what had happened to him, he was in his new home where he would stay till Christmas or New Year's butchering. "Why sure," said Zack, "it don't take much strength if you got the brains."

It made me think of the Ralph Waldo Emerson story of the calf with set legs that wouldn't go into the barn, and Emerson pushing and pulling and getting nowhere; when along comes Henry Thoreau, puts his finger in the calf's mouth, and leads it in with the merest crook of his arm.

Autumns after that, we looked forward to the hog-transferring business. It was quite fun to grab the curly tail and steer that obstinate stern with such ease and savoir faire.

The kids are taking to the farm like ducks to water. I was afraid the farm life might make drugstore cowboys out of them, as so often happens. Sue said to me the other day, "Oh Dad, wouldn't it be nice if we didn't have a car! Oh gee it would be nice, 'n' I'd have a little red horse then, 'n' you'd have a big horse, 'n' we could go riding along."

"What about Mother?"

"Mother would ride on your big horse with you, 'n' we'd all go joggin' along . . ."

It wouldn't be such a bad idea if I followed my daughter's suggestion and gave up cars, or even went a bit farther and took the roads afoot without a horse. If I walk far enough and aimlessly enough, if I poke my nose into a sufficient number of stray corners and get bitten by a sufficient number of irritable farm dogs, I'll run into enough stories so I can buy a horse apiece for each of the family, including the two boys, and we'll all go jogging along.

Austen keeps asking questions. Why is the world round? Which is the front side and which is the back side? Why does the sun rise in front of the house and set in the back? When I try to answer, he thinks up a new one and doesn't listen to the old explanation—not that it's very clear. Does God look in the window at me when I'm asleep to see if I put my pajamas on like mother told me to? Does the devil look in too? Which did God make first, Adam or Eve? and did they have a baby or did God make the baby too?

Kay says that when she was little her brothers and sisters used to ask her father, "Who did Adam's son marry?" and her father used to say, "Oh, he went to China and married a China girl."

A very good answer too.

Our neighbor, Lane Kent, from over the hill, came wandering along the road the other day, and he was feeling low. "I hope winter'll soon be done. My boots is wore out and my mittens turned to rags. My cut's done for and my britches is out at the knees. Crimus, I had to put on an old suit of underwear with sleeves only *that* long. Last night I about froze in bed."

I suppose it is permissible for me to smile at my neighbors a little. They laugh at me plenty, don't worry, when they see me, horseless, carrying firewood around on my back, transplanting trees, fixing up my house before I fix my barn, and other ridiculousnesses. Luckily for them, they don't publish their little jokes, so there is no rancor.

Kay has gone off for the afternoon to the Ladies' Missionary Society meeting, leaving me to minister to the souls and bodies of my own little tribe of heathens. Kay doesn't believe in religious missions, only in medical and an occasional, miraculous, intelligent, economic or educational mission. But there are few sociable diversions in winter. I think she enjoys very much this serious and solemn preoccupation with distant savages on the part of just an average lot of humans who can't begin to run their own lives.

28

ONE DAY Zack came and wanted us to drive him in the car to a neighboring town to see a lawyer. He had a penchant for small-scale law suits anyway, so I was a little balky at first. But it was about the terrible Ceelie, and he said he'd *got* to go and see if his lawyer couldn't arrange a meeting with her to decide about the furniture and stuff she claimed from him. The idea that she would come someday when he was away and burn his house down was an unending tribulation to him, and he had to get rid of it some-how. I didn't want to go, but he had been so extremely helpful about lending us his horses and tools and coming at most any hour of the day or night, I couldn't refuse, just this once.

It turned out to be but the first of many many trips. We would drive off somewhere, often of a Sunday afternoon, to Barton or Newport or Morrisville or somewhere, Kay and I and the kids and Zack. He had an appointment with some lawyer, and while he was talking with his legal expert, we would stroll around. It usually took him a very long time too, because he could seldom start right in talking directly about anything, but must sneak up on the subject obliquely from various angles. Repeatedly his lawyers tried to arrange a meeting with Ceelie at their offices (to which we conveyed Zack) but Ceelie never came.

We were getting pretty sick of this—almost as desperate as Zack. I hadn't supposed that another man's ex-wife could trouble me so much, but that's the way it is in the country. I was so desperate

I had just about decided that the next time Zack asked his inevitable question, upon our arrival home, "Well, how much do I owe ye?" I would reply, "Ten dollars, please." That would fix him, neighbor or no neighbor.

But about this time he finally dug up a really clever lawyer—only thirty miles way—who began to go into the situation with a fine-tooth comb.

"He's onto something, that Lawyer Stiles. He's goin' to find something, I believe," said Zack in his most wonderfully secretive way. "He's got mor'n one man out of trouble."

"I thought it was girls that got into trouble, Zack."

"No, it's men that get into trouble." He nodded his old white head sagely. "The girls are too smart for us." The saintly smile of resignation would have done justice to an angel. If I hadn't known that he was at this time chasing a girl of nineteen, whose pregnancy he had already accomplished, I would have been much impressed. All the way home he sang in a minor discord his favorite love song, "Over the Garden Wall." There was also the touching ballad, "Someday I'll Have My Title Free and Clear."

Not long after, he came trotting briskly over in his buggy. We heard the usual "Whoa!" out on the front lawn and next came Zack hopping over the nigh front wheel with a letter clutched aloft. It was from Lawyer Stiles, of course. "Ceelie's got no claim on me at all," Zack shouted. "We was never married in the first place. 'Tweren't legal. Not a stick of furniture, mind ye."

It seemed that in his researches Lawyer Stiles had unearthed some pertinent data. When Zack married Ceelie, she had not long been divorced from a former mate. Vermont law, unlike that of Nevada, requires a two-year wait after divorce before remarriage is legal. They had been married in Vermont after a wait of only a year and a half, so it didn't hold.

"Why, Zack Tyler," said Kay, "my, my, you were living in sin all that time, weren't you."

" 'Tain't sin if you don't know it," Zack happily replied.

189

We were quite happy too that there would be no more lawyer trips.

Even Ceelie, the redoubtable Ceelie, was affected. She had merely been separated from Zack during the long period while she lived here and there attracting and discarding males. Now she immediately married some poor devil from New Hampshire and moved way over there beyond the Connecticut Lakes. We never heard of her again, and shed no tears over that.

There remained, however, the matter of nineteen-year-old Lubie and her approaching child. Lubie went to work at Zack's as his housekeeper—that fine and salty designation. After her child was born and had attained an age for attending social functions all done up in an embroidered bonnet, Lubie and Zack were married. It was a quiet but impressive ceremony at the Congregational Church. Zack was dressed in a fine old black broadcloth Sunday-go-to-meeting suit that looked twice as formal as a cutaway. He was on his best behavior, replete with saintly smile, respectful dignity and fatherly concern for the bride. He adjusted himself so inconspicuously to the bizarre sex rites and quaint marriage customs of this particular tribe at this particular time in history in this particular part of the globe, you would never have dreamed— to watch him nibble a cake at the reception—that there was so much of the old Adam in him.

Kay was apparently not impressed either by the sacredness of the bond whose solemnization we had just witnessed, for halfway home she remarked for no special reason, " 'Tain't sin if you don't know it."

29

At the start we used to do our gardening correctly, oh perfectly. There was a chapter in the garden books called Preparing the Soil. You needed at least three inches of humus mulch spread just so. You should chemically test every square inch of your plot. You should lay out your garden like an architect building a fourteen-room house. You should spend at least three days staking your tomatoes, and as for telephone peas—they were likely to get ripe on you before you finished building the fancy fence for them to climb on. We used to go to the woods across the road with a wheelbarrow and bring home leaf mould and swamp muck, and we even used to experiment with different kinds of litter from under different species of trees. Please don't misunderstand me. I am a great believer in compost and in mulching and in organic gardening. But I don't believe in fussiness for fussiness' sake. Even organic gardening techniques have to be translated into terms that will not bankrupt you.

We used to plant our bean seeds exactly three inches apart in the row and go back spacing them more evenly before we covered them up. We used to plant exactly six seeds in every hill of corn and stand and wonder whether seven may be too much. We always planted our rows precisely eight or thirteen inches apart, according to what the books said.

The garden books. The equipment. The label tags. The gloves. The advice. Oh meticulous.

Now, I like gardening. I love to stand with my bare feet in the warm earth and hear the corn leaves rustle. I like the harrowing and the planting and the first radishes and the last big heads of cabbage with their odd and beautifully-shaped leaves of green. I love to pare a raw potato and eat it. Raw corn is also good if you chew it long enough. I even like the stain that pulling kale brings to my hands, and especially the sharp and diverse smells of vegetative juices. I'm not so sure that animals are superior to vegetables. Our vegetables have never been just a mass marketable commodity to me—a ton of redness, a ton of greenness. Silly as it seems, the individual golden bantam ears, the fluted leaf of a Chinese cabbage, or the luscious soft smoothness of a ripe tomato have always seemed like individual works of art to me.

But I don't like fussiness and unnecessary work. It took us years to learn to garden right. We used to approach the problem as though we were building a suspension bridge, and that took half the joy out of it. Gradually we discovered that it doesn't matter very much whether you plant bean seeds two inches apart or four. If you get the right amount of rain and sunshine, you'll have more beans than you can use. If, on the other hand, you get too little or too much of either, chances are that neither one of them will come up anyhow, and you could have spilled in a handful for all the difference it made. We made a new garden spot way out in the field where there wasn't any witch grass. We gave up measuring with a ruler "one-fourth to one-eighth inch deep." And one of the best things we gave up was planting rows eight inches apart or thirteen inches apart. Most of the garden books are written for people who haven't much land, and so they crowd their rows. It's on account of this that they advise close rows, squash and melon beds here and there, some rows crosswise, some rows lengthwise till you achieve that fourteen-room house affect. We gradually evolved and got some sense. We planted all rows two-and-a-half or three feet apart. We had plenty of room to plant them ten feet apart if we had cared to. All our rows ran lengthwise of our long and narrow garden plot. Every ten days we borrowed a horse from Zack and horse-cultivated the whole plot, thus accomplishing in half an hour what would have required two full days of hoeing. We gave up staking our tomatoes and let them ramble around, the way the commercial growers do. What if a few did rot, resting on the ground? We had more than we could use. The books said it was a wonderful idea to carry bushels of green tomatoes in the fall up to some dark attic and spread them on the floor to ripen. We did this too. It was a tall job, and every one of those tomatoes rotted on the floor of that dark attic and had to be carried down again, which was an even taller job. Not being very bright, I did this for three years. Then I gave it up for life. The books say that you should transplant all your tomatoes out of your cold-frame into your garden at such and such a time. So we did. Years later we discovered that in this northern clime it is highly advantageous to *leave* six or eight of the young tomato plants right in the cold-frame where they are. This is the sort of thing that is too easy for the garden books; that wouldn't be any fun for them. But the tomato plants in the cold-frame, undisturbed and warm, are about three weeks ahead of the garden plants, which have been slowed down by transplanting (usually two transplantings, one to pots and again to the garden). The cold-frame tomatoes ripen and are edible in early August, whereas the garden plants often don't bear till the first of September.

The children have become good helpers too and seem to like gardening, with occasional reservations. By some happy accident we got them off on the right foot when it came to gardening. When they were very little and in the garden with us, it was quite natural to say, "Now you mustn't pull those weeds, because you can's tell weeds from onions and you'll pull up the good plants." This naturally elicted the reply, "Yes I can too. Look." Ditto with planting, which they now particularly enjoy. "Let me plant a few seeds," they used to say when they could hardly talk. And we'd reply, "Well, here are just a few," and we'd drop a half dozen into that tiny palm. In a couple of minutes back came the small hand for "More, let me put in just a few more." It is natural for the younger ones to want to do what the older ones can. And so planting is fun for us all now, and I hope it will always be.

"Mother, shall I do three rows of weeding or four?"

"Oh, four if you like."

"Susan can't push the cultivator. She isn't big enough."

"Oh yes I am."

Mother says, "Why don't you just pull weeds, Sue."

The little girl looks up, so earnest, brown eyes beseeching, and lisps from toothless front gums, "Pleathe."

"Oh, all right."

Proudly she scratches down a half a row, tanned barefoot, a part of the family.

As I look back, the whole philosophy of our gardening has changed. We used to be so afraid we weren't doing each step right, according to the books, and we went at it from the basis of a maximum of work and a minimum of food. Now we have learned to be selective, and we know that there are a great many fancy techniques that just simply do not pay. We never thin a weedy row of carrots, for instance, where the carrots are few and far between, as we used to. We just hoe the thing up and plant it again. It is much quicker and ten times as effective, if eating carrots is the object. We now get more with less work instead of less with more work. I should imagine the proportions are about twice as much produce with about half as much work. And that leaves more time for sunbathing in the corn rows, munching on a raw turnip, one's head pillowed on a pumpkin, which is an important phase of gardening that the books do not mention.

It is canning time and everybody at our house is very busy. The stove is perking hard all day long and the big kettles of vegetables and quart jars boil and steam. We find that for some products big two-quart jars save a lot of work; some other things that are used in small quantities are most effectively canned in pints. The boiling takes a lot of split wood.

"Eat what you can, and what you can't, can," is the watchword, now our garden is flourishing. Late into the evening we all sit out on the grass at a table overlooking the lake, stringing bushels of beans and shelling telephone peas.

We will have so many beans we'll never be able to can them all. But that will be all right; we'll just let whole rows of them mature, then pull up the vines and pile them on the barn floor, where we'll thrash them for baking beans in the autumn when we get more time. We find that any kind of string beans, if left to get old, make good baking beans, whether the seed is black, brown, red or white. But the best are a big brown kind with a light spot, called yellow-eye. With browned pork, some onion, a dash of maple sugar and plenty of seasoning, we'll have many a dish of baked beans this coming year, and they no more resemble the baked beans in cans than a young broiler fried in butter resembles boiled old hen. Kay soaks the beans all night, then simmers and bakes the mixture all day gently on a low fire. The final product mustn't be too wet, and mustn't be too dry, but when it's just right the pot liquor alone is as tasty as wine.

We find telephone peas are best, in spite of the fact that they must have something to climb on and the labor of bushing them or making a fence is great and onerous. Bushing the peas is always a job I dislike. But I have learned to make a simple fence of chicken wire, and that lightens the task. We have a collection of good fence posts in the garden, keep them there all the time, drive them into the pea row in the spring, hook the roll of chicken wire onto shingle nails in the posts, stretching by hand as we go. We plant a thick double row of peas four inches each side of the fence, and on the wire they get the sun both sides and ripen by the bushel. In comparison with dwarf unbushed peas, we find we get about fives times as many telephone peas from our five-foot-high fence, and they are bigger and better-tasting and easier to handle. In the fall we unhook the wire from the posts and roll it up. Then we pull the posts and pile them beside the garden. Stupid as it sounds, it has taken me years to evolve this simple system. I used to hire a wagon and go and cut birch brush from a woodlot where piles of it remained from a firewood cutting. Loading it in the wagon was almost impossible, the brush is so springy. Most of it is too small, and in order to stick it in the ground you have to make a hole first with a crowbar. Even so, some of it topples over in the wind when the peas get heavy. Bushing the peas is one of the old-fashioned arts we have discarded with relish. When we first began to use chicken wire, I used to staple it into the posts, then in the fall I'd pull the posts, lay the whole collection flat, and roll it up, posts and all. This gave me an unwieldy mass of posts and wire too heavy to lift, snarled in weeds and trash. In the spring I had to pull all the staples out and get the wire off the posts to make anything like a tight fence anyhow. Discarding the staples has made pea-growing 100 per cent simpler.

The corn comes on, and we just about live on the young golden ears, picked fresh, cooked five minutes later, eaten twenty minutes after they left the stalk. They also are very different from the usual product. Sometimes at evenings we roast them in their husks in an open fire or in the ashpan of the stove, and the taste is so wild and sweet it makes you think of Indian days. Each morning we marvel at the abundance of our garden, the parsley, onions, beets, carrots, cabbage, lettuce, swiss chard, pumpkins, the acorn squashes, hubbard squashes, berries, rutabagas, tomatoes—all in such profusion as to be practically worthless. Stray armfuls of the stuff lie on the ground rotting, or we feed them to the pig. And this is food for which people hunger!

Everyone knows that what ails our economy is the distribution system and the great spread between producer and consumer. It looks to me as though the way to beat that is to provide certain easily produced necessities, such as vegetables, for yourself. We often wonder about the canners' ads that speak of large-scale savings and quantity-production perfection. We wonder about the efficiency of chain stores too. Not that they do not perform a service for helpless ones. They do, and naturally one must buy if one does not produce. But why be a helpless one if one can avoid it?

We have found that the only time we lose money on our farm work is when we raise stuff to sell. When we eat it ourselves we get it for less than we could buy. We are our own best market. We are so far from other good-sized markets that, of course, we are at a disadvantage when it comes to selling. Probably the smartest thing we could do to make a profit on our farm would be to build a few summer cottages to rent, and thus import our own market. As it is, we find that when we try to sell stuff, we often receive less than the stuff cost us. I remember taking fifteen dozen ears of fresh golden bantam corn to a chain store to sell. They offered me five cents a dozen, though they were reselling for twenty-five cents a dozen. I brought my corn home and fed it to the pig, and was very glad I had a pig who would so enthusiastically grow pork for me. Of course, when trying to keep account of costs (which we never do), we don't figure our time at anything very much. This is because we've never been able to make an estimate of what our time is worth, and we immediately jump out of the realm of mathematics into philosophy. If we weren't raising food and canning it, we'd be going to movies and building swimming pools, wouldn't we? All we can make of it is that we are happily constituted so that raising food makes us strong and happy and gives us aesthetic delight as well as gustatory pleasure. So we've decided we had better take advantage of it, and that's that.

We are constantly experimenting with ways and means of minimizing the disadvantages of our late, short growing season. There is no end to the early growth one can get from cold frames, hot beds, hot caps, simple sash greenhouses, early gardens in the shelter of south-facing stone walls, and so on. What we are trying to figure out is how we can grow early stuff for ourselves in the simplest, cheapest way. We do not need any great quantity of forced-growth stuff—just enough to keep us going till the garden comes on. Next year we are going to have another and special hotbed where we raise plants for eating, not transplanting. These particular plants will stay where they are and not be slowed by transplanting. They'll grow faster in their special, warm place. By the time they grow so tall they touch the glass, the weather will be warm enough to leave the glass off entirely anyhow. In this way, I think, we'll have tomatoes, lettuce, chinese cabbage, leeks, and swiss chard in early July or late June.

One of the simplest ways to start early plants is in an old tub or barrel half filled with earth and covered or partially covered by a pane of glass.

Our long winter has many disadvantages, but there are advantages too. Most of our winter food crop does not ripen until cool weather in the fall, and that simplifies the problem of storage. In more southerly regions the best vegetable crop is over by early August, let us say, so that any un-canned products soon spoil in the heat. The books will tell you that the thing to do in such case is to make second and third plantings, late, for winter storage. But few amateurs have luck with late plantings in the hot dry summer months. The weeds have a tremendous start on everything late in the season and tend to crowd out all your seedlings. Even though you harrow the piece, the weeds come first. We've never had much luck with late second plantings, and I don't think most amateurs do either.

Winter comes, and our cupboard shelves in the snug stone cellar are an art gallery of crimson and green and brown and white jars. We have canned raspberries, blueberries, peas, beans, a few beets, some apple sauce from windfalls, grape jelly, fifty quarts of canned yellow corn, many quarts of beef stew and beef soup stock, also pork. A five-gallon keg of cider sits in the corner. In a wooden bin are twelve bushels of fine Green Mountain potatoes, and we have bought three barrels of apples. Our rutabagas, most of our beets and carrots are stored in layers of sand. There are bushels of onions and a hundred Danish Ball Head cabbages laid out on rough shelves. The cellar stays at about thirty-four degrees all winter, and our cabbages, apples and other raw stuff keep fresh and firm until May.

All in all, our cellar is one of our prime assets of independence, and I can never understand how so many families have given up this important factor in living. As soon as you give up your cellar or warm the whole space with a furnace, you have lost your storage space and made yourself a victim of the small-package racket— "Eleven ounces, 36¢, Special Sale." Often sixty cents of every dollar you spend for food will be going for colored ink, cellophane, promotion, and freight, none of which you can eat. As soon as you have no cellar, you cannot purchase by the barrel and the bushel and the gallon and the case at the psychological moment when the stuff is plentiful. In winter we often go down to the cellar and contemplate the art gallery. When a blizzard is howling outside is the best time.

30

Sue and I have been chopping wood all the winter's afternoon up on the hill. There is a weak crust on the snow, and Sue is so tiny and light she can run around on top of it, laughing at me while I plow in fluff almost to the waist. I am thinning out some birches and hemlocks and firs from among a young stand of sugar maples up on the hill to give them more room and sunlight, to encourage them so that someday we'll have a fair-sized sugar bush. Fortunately there are thirty or forty young maples big enough to hang buckets on already, and that is enough for me to play around with at sugaring time to make a family supply for our griddle cakes. For some of the other young maples no bigger than my wrist the "someday" is a good many years off, and I can hardly expect to live to see the day when they are sizable. Sugar maples grow slowly, and it takes sixty or eighty years to make a big one. Nevertheless, it gives me great happiness to have a part.

Little Sue and I roam around in the snow, carrying axes, saw, wedges, laying our hands on this young tree and that one. She has her own tiny axe, quite dull as yet. But gradually I am making it sharper as she gets accustomed to using it. The below-freezing air is crystal-lovely, and the sunshine has a two-o'clockish slant. The sunny-still, ten-above-zero air feels pleasantly mild to us. We both have good boots, double mittens, snug ear-lap caps, and doubtless that has something to do with our complacence.

"This is a good one," I say, looking up at the crown of a young maple.

Sue squints up along the trunk critically, laying her button nose against the bark. "Yes, this is a good one."

"Why do we keep lugging these axes and saws around, Sue?"

"I don't know."

"Let's put them down."

"Let's put them down."

When a man thinks of trees, he thinks of his age. It's like the bittersweetness and the life-and-death-ness of so many natural things. Here are generations of humans tangled in these generations of maples. Old Uncle Hank got poor a long time ago and cut most all the big maples down. But there were young ones, and new sprouts came too. Fortunately for me, this was a poor woodland pasture, much grown up, practically no grass, and so the cows, although they were free to roam up here, seldom came. If the cows had pastured in these woods, they'd have eaten all the little maple shoots. They'll eat little maples as readily as clover. It is a common thing in these Vermont sugar places where the big trees stand far apart and the grass is good that there are no young maples coming on. The big trees at one hundred years or so begin to die at the crowns. Their tough and whitening limbs lie on the green grass like bones, along with rotting chunks of tops that have fallen. And there are no young ones to take their places.

Fortunately, a few people are beginning to realize how sad it is to mine the past and leave the present poor. And it is a growing practice, and a good one, to fence cows out of woodlands where they do so much damage to get so little feed. The majority of people, however, don't do anything about sugar maples. It takes a lifetime to do much with them, and then what? Then you are dead.

But supposing in your lifetime you made some grow and got great happiness out of seeing them grow? That is just lucky for somebody else, I guess.

Anyhow, Sue and I like it. And we'll get half our next year's firewood out of the thinnings. Our consciences begin to hurt us because we aren't getting any work done. So we get busy chopping and sawing and making the chips fly, laying down the "wolf" firs and the overstory birches. Sue can worry a little limb off a fir sometimes, and likes to stick them up in the snow and play with them. Far off we hear another axe ringing in the winter afternoon, and it is as though the two axes spoke to each other.

We must figure out where the sled road will go for the team, and make it wind away from the steepest banks. We pile our wood accordingly, keeping it in mind that when we hire Lane Kent's team he does not like to drive a heavy load down steep grades.

It is nice that we have our own firewood, our own cedar fence posts, our own maples, our own rocks to build walls with. Some of the valley farms can't say as much.

Sue is singing a little song to herself, rather tuneless and quite incomprehensible to anyone else. But at least it is original. My one-man crosscut jumps a bit in the cut and does not run overly well, but it is seldom you can get a saw filed and set perfectly, and even then it does not stay that way very long. I am used to it, and its curved, worn wooden handle seems used to me. By-and-by we have half a cord or so cut and piled.

Susan starts to whimper and says, "My feets cold." So we decide we'll make a little lean-to and a fire in front of it. We dig out the snow and throw in fir brush to sit on. A pole between two low-limbed firs is our ridge. Balsam fir branches from our cutting are everywhere, and we stack them thick all around for roof and sides. Dead branches whose needles have turned red ignite like torches, and we throw on some more dead ones, crawl into our nook and take off Sue's boots. "Oh boy this is fun," she says, curling her toes. "Tell me a story."

Telling stories isn't chopping wood or thinning maples. But after all, you only live once. So I tell her a very short one about a little boy who got lost in the woods in winter, but, fortunately, he knew how to take care of himself. He had his little axe, of course, and he made himself a snug lean-to and built a fire, and he tried not to be lonely in the night when he heard the owls hooting, and when he began to freeze, he just built up the fire. So, in the morning he looked around at a few hills and trees and things and saw where the sun rose up, and he decided he knew where he was, so he struck off for home and got there just in time for dinner. His pa and ma were mighty glad to see him too. His mother made some pancakes to see how many he could eat, and he ate ten without syrup and another ten with, and they all lived happily ever after.

"Why don't you write a book about that?" Sue said. But I had to chop some more wood. So she sat by the warm embers putting on her boots wrong foot to while I cut and piled a few more firs to raise my afternoon's rather meager tally. We always set out to do about twice as much as we accomplish, Sue and I. But we usually have a good time. Possibly it is because she is at the most cooperative stage of her entire life. I'll be kind of sorry when she grows old enough to go to school.

31

Yᴇsᴛᴇʀᴅᴀʏ we went over to Gorham's cottage at Shadow Lake. Early in the morning while the dew was sparkling on the grass Kim and I started out to walk it, twelve miles by the little roads, while the rest of the family came by car.

When you walk, on the dirt, on the gravel, over the brooks, past the wide sunny hayfields, dipping down through the glens, round the bends, crossing the high ridges and looking back at the range on range of hills, wading a brook and looking at frogs under stones, you realize how intensely lovely the world is. I don't think there's country anywhere in the world for rambles like this northern Vermont region. There are many old roads with grass in the middle, seldom used or completely gullied out so as to be passable only afoot. And the smells of hay in the upland fields, of hollyhocks by an immaculately kept huge white farmhouse, of mint in a glen, and fresh running water over the yellow sand, the strong scent of alders, of maple-arched avenues roofing a mile-long hill, of abandoned farmhouses where the pale perfume of weathered old wood and ancient manure-piles and thistles and roses blend in an essence of forsakenness.

When our feet got tired, we took off our shoes and walked barefoot on the two smooth tracks of roads where tires of cars had whisked away the gravel. Here the road was ice-cold in a shady damp hollow; there in the sun as warm as a sweaty brow. You know what your senses are for when you walk these morning roads, through the sugar places, by the pastures where red and white Guernsey heifers trot along inside the fences for a spell to keep you company, and at the fence corner where their way is barred they stand breathing light moo's—beautiful, pitiful dopes whose sorrow is not very sad.

We were headed east, and as nearly always happens in Vermont, we found the east-west roads were few, and smaller and narrower than the north-south routes. The east roads were so few, we had to go like steps, with a mile jog north to get a little road east over the ridge, and a mile jog south in the next valley to strike another eastbound track over the next ridge. It's the ice age, I suppose, that grooved the north-south valleys where the highways wind beside the streams, following the gentler slopes. But the hill roads running east over the ridges, the little crooked tracks where the ruts are shining brooks,—they're the narrow and exciting ones. They're the ones where you part the spider webs as you walk in the morning. You feel the light silk touch on your wrist and face, and as you break the gossamer, you're breaking some very heavy chains that bound you. And they bound you utterly needlessly, all because you haven't been out swinging along the hill roads in the morning for ever so long.

We got to talking in order to pass the time when the way seemed long. We wondered why the brook in the last little valley was running north, while the brook in a parallel valley ran south. But from a rise we could size up the lay of the land and figure it out pretty well.

By-and-by we grew very weary and lay in the grass by a stone wall under a big maple tree, watching four men on a golden slope pitch hay. We could hear the tractor snorting along, and the ring of hayfork tines on tines. And we leaned back limp as rags, for we'd already covered seven miles, and we thought it grand to watch them sweat.

By-and-by we got the rhythm and crossed the crest of a magnificent high ridge whence we could look back and see the Green

Mountain chain spread out like wallpaper for us: Camel's Hump, Mansfield, Eden, Jay Peak. And we went down a long, long hill, past a sweet farmhouse all scented and tinted with marigolds and petunias, flocks, zinnias, and asters, a farm called COZY BEND with the Z backwards, and on down a narrowing evergreen valley till we saw Shadow Lake in the bottom like a Promised Land.

A farmer and his wife bound for town picked us up the last half mile in a new Ford—a feeblish man with a wife the epitome of all farmers' wives. They stopped at a neighbor's to ask if there were any errands in the village. "Can't remember the name of that plaster nohow. And you made a pie of that mess of raspberries, did you? I was wondering how it came out, I said to Horace just last evening. You heard from Jed? Well I thought likely you'd have heard yestd'y but I declare I was just too busy. Horace brought in a heifer with one tit got cut on the wire and I declare we were half the night a-doctorin' her."

Horace: "Yes and you'd never believe it, but she's going to be all right. Well—"

The women were still at it, so he put the car in gear and broke their conversation in the only possible way, apologetically, but it had to be done. His wife seemed to be used to it.

The Gorhams saw us get out of the car in front of their place— it was just about noon—and they gave us the razz and claimed we had ridden the whole way. We didn't mind. The lake was at our feet crying to be swum in, so we obliged.

Mr. Gorham is a textbook sales manager for a big publisher. You'd never know it when he's on vacation. He has a shack of a little cottage built half over the water, and every winter the frost humps it into new bumps and sags that never fail to delight him. He's always carpentering at it in a crude but pleasant sort of way, knocking down partitions, putting new ones up, making cupboards in the corners and hidden shelves among the two-by-four studs, where he conceals odd boxes of screws and old hand-forged wagon irons and peavy-hooks that he's picked up and has no use for

206

whatever. He had a new electric water pump. Every time anybody turned on the faucet, the pump began to run. He would cock his ear and listen to it, and if it changed its hum the slightest bit he'd look as worried as though the world were coming to an end. We all laughed at him and had a wonderful time. Lacking a screen door for the back door, they had only a curtain of gauze hung up; it was short, too, leaving a space at least a foot wide underneath it. He couldn't bother with that. He was busy outside building a stairway of flat rocks down to the water's edge. He told me that the main thing he liked about the house was that it was such an impromptu contraption he could alter it any way he liked without hurting it. "If I ever get it just right to suit me," he said, "it won't be any fun, and I'll sell it and start on another one." By the look of it we decided it would never be just right, so he is probably pretty safe.

We had a wonderful big dinner, with twelve people at the table, including his grown son and a handsome blond daughter who is married to a sailor now away on a merchant ship. She had just received a letter that morning from her husband in Port Said, and he was bound home. The letter stuck up in her breast pocket like a talisman.

Mr. Gorham was raised in the Pacific northwest. For hours we lay in the grass, while the rest of them pitched horseshoes, and he told me about the Lewis and Clark expedition up the Missouri River and down the Clearwater, Snake, Columbia to the Pacific, and what a good way it would be to teach children geography, following such journeys, their uncertainties, their adventures, the mountain passes they searched out, the Indian tribes they met, the lay of the land, and the cities that have grown up on their camp sites.

In the evening we had a campfire and sang. There was a boy with an accordion who played surprisingly well. Late in the night we drove home. The stars were out bright, and the children fell sound asleep in the back seat on the way.

32

DURING THE WAR we could not stay on the farm. The war dislocated us, like everybody else. We had no desire to stay at the farm, and our own private battle seemed temporarily on the shelf, because it was at stake. We wanted to be usful, and so we tried, but whether we succeeded or not, I wouldn't know. We bounced around here and there like a good many other millions, doing what we could, grateful to have any sort of roof that wasn't being perforated by bombs, living always on too intimate terms with our neighbors' trash and garbage cans, yet living without any real certainty that we had a right to live at all.

At last the time came when we were bound back for the farm, one hot day in August, 1945. To us the 410 miles up from New York City seemed a long grind, and even after we reached the south end of Vermont, we had more than 150 miles to go. Just at sunset we were rolling up the last stretch of road, seeing the quiet lake again, the maple trees and the white gable end of our house gleaming among the leaves.

We pulled up and tumbled onto the green grass beside the house, where we stretched out flat and pressed our noses into the green cool freshness of the grass roots. It was too good even to speak of. The sun sank down behind the western ridges across the lake, the bright blue of the sky dimmed, and it almost seemed we could feel the coolness of the dew quietly falling like a blessing. In that moment Kay and I were conscious of all the millions who had died. Kim lifted up his chin and rested it in his palm, staring in disbelief at the rolling profile of Albany hills. "You know," he said, "those hills are in my mind."

In the time we'd been away I had often thought of their distinctive shape myself and of the many times they had been blue when I was coming home. I lay in the grass, wondering about the future and what it would bring us, now that we were home again.

Only time and the needs of a family can determine whether we'll be able to stay on our farm year-round or summers only, or whether we'll find ourselves looking for another small farm somewhere else, now that we've learned a little about it the hard way. Perhaps it doesn't matter. The sunset will still flame over the snowdrifts, and the beautiful blizzards will come roaring in from the northwest. The trees will lose their leaves and grow them again. The cowslips will spring up in the swales and the violets in the woods. And in me and in my children, I hope, will be a consciousness that natural things are as powerful and all-pervading as they ever were in the time of the pagan Greeks and the wine-dark sea and the sylvan gods. The springtimes come, when the maple leaves unroll "as big as a mouse's ear"; the wild roses bloom; the blackberries ripen; and these things will go on, as the old New England land deeds phrase it, "as long as grass grows and water runs." It is good to know all this, for there is really nothing else.

Books from The Countryman Press

A selection of our books on the history and culture of New England: